Heavy Metal Music in Argentina

Heavy Metal Music in Argentina

In Black We Are Seen

EDITED BY

Emiliano Scaricaciottoli, Nelson Varas-Díaz, and Daniel Nevárez Araújo

intellect

Bristol, UK / Chicago, USA

First published in the UK in 2020 by
Intellect, The Mill, Parnall Road, Fishponds, Bristol, BS16 3JG, UK

First published in the USA in 2020 by
Intellect, The University of Chicago Press, 1427 E. 60th Street,
Chicago, IL 60637, USA

Copyright © 2020 Intellect Ltd
Paperback edition © 2023 Intellect Ltd

First edition published in Spanish in 2016 by
Ediciones La Parte Maldita

All rights reserved. No part of this publication may be reproduced, stored in a retrieval system, or transmitted, in any form or by any means, electronic, mechanical, photocopying, recording, or otherwise, without written permission.

A catalogue record for this book is available from the British Library.

Copy editor: MPS Technologies
Cover designer: Aleksandra Szumlas
Cover image: Kadriel Betsen and Daniel López Miranda – Cuneiform Creative Agency
Production manager: Laura Christopher
Typesetting: Contentra Technologies

Hardback ISBN 9-781-7-89382-990
Paperback ISBN 9-781-7-89387-483
ePDF ISBN 9-781-7-89383-003
ePUB ISBN 9-781-7-89383-010

To find out about all our publications, please visit
www.intellectbooks.com.
There, you can subscribe to our e-newsletter,
browse or download our current catalogue,
and buy any titles that are in print.

Contents

Preface to the Second Edition

Group for Interdisciplinary Research on Argentinian Heavy Metal (GIIHMA)

The Argentinean metal aficionado who replicates and repeats – as a liturgical exercise, simply because it is what is right in an act of faith – the words of the artist-creator usually earns the punishment from the literati. Atheists and believers. Well-bred governors and sorrowful servants. The consortium that comprises the national heavy metal music world – by all means debatable, but, to our understanding, real – has undertaken an inner battle (sometimes silent, sometimes ear-piercing) about what should be done with the future of our movement. Making the movement 'ours' was the foremost challenge of the GIIHMA. We knew that the Spanish edition of *Heavy Metal Music in Argentina* (2016) would bring forth debates, rifts, appropriations, and wrath. But we did not foresee that the book and the collective itself would bring together a sizable group of young men and women who, aside from expending themselves in the dynamic pogo dance, would find the energy to rethink themselves within the hungry mass of the concert space, in that dark alley that still feeds the morbid desire for isolation, in the street corner which has become such a masculine space that it has turned rotten, cowardly, and homicidal. *Heavy Metal Music in Argentina* was a 'movement' within a larger movement, made dynamic by the threat of its own disappearance (of leaders and referents experiencing decay), aching due to its rifts, its dead ones, its absences. We did not come here discreetly; we came to fulfill our destiny: to defend, question, and critique Argentinean heavy metal's work, fundamentally the work of Ricardo Iorio, its greatest proponent. And because we are believers, we will venture to say that this book has been a triumph. And whoever reads these words will know what we are talking about.

Following the distribution of the first 500 copies in its Spanish version, the challenge is, without a doubt, much greater. It is to avoid fragmentation, to avoid separation. Argentinean heavy metal is riddled with such stories. We hope that this second edition in English will replicate, in quality and quantity, the spaces in which Argentinean heavy metal can express itself. We must also add that between the first and second edition there was a trajectory, an effort and movement already inscribed in our foundational manifesto: to federalize (ourselves). For the second year in a row we stormed the Book Fair in La Rural, participating in the Heavy Metal Book Fair at the Zona Futuro stand, an opportunity that arose thanks to the support and persistence of Gito Minore and María Inés Martínez. The book was also presented in Mü Punto de Encuentro, at the Centro Cultural de la Cooperación, at the Asamblea de Flores, in Puerto Madryn, and in Mar del Plata. Extending our reach, GIIHMA's works made their way into the newspaper Andén, and further spread their wings through the activities set up by our workmates at the UADER (Universidad Autónoma de Entre Ríos) – who offered the university course 'Rock: Between counterculture and cultural market' (FHAyCS, Paraná Campus) – and Nelson Varas-Díaz, professor and writer at the Florida International University.

Issuing our book through publisher La Parte Maldita also helped us enormously, as far as territorial reach is concerned. Suddenly, Catamarca, Córdoba, Chubut, Neuquén, Río Negro, and other corners of our homeland were discussing *Heavy Metal Music in Argentina*. And among those debates, a fundamental one was born: how do we promote the emergence of new action groups that will then foster the involvement of metal aficionados as well as the adoption of metal activities among new groups, thus encouraging the latter to write amongst/in/with Argentinean heavy metal?

We would like to express our appreciation to Luciano Sáliche (Infobae), Javier Knario Compiano (Vórterix), Luis Hitoshi Díaz (Radio Led), Daniel Cafferata Soto, and Pablo Gadea (Café Metal), and so many new voices for their efforts in spreading this work and for risking so much so that GIIHMA can enjoy a few minutes on mass media.

We would like to also affirm our deepest commitment to the former students of the course we imparted at University of Buenos Aires (for the second year in a row), and to our fellow comrades of Raza Trunka who stirred up the prudish campus of Filosofía y Letras.

A toast to La Parte Maldita for seeking out the greatest heretics and placing your trust in us, in a year in which the rope has tightened around our necks, as they try to paralyze our cultural, political, and economical endeavors. Here is your homework: resist.

Foreword

Emiliano Scaricaciottoli

Reckoning

Usually, in academic slang, when we stumble onto the absence of a particular content or curricular space, we say that we have a 'vacancy area'. To enter into a vacancy is to find the best sale. It is also to find the highest demand. It is magical proof of an empty desire. How much has there been written about Argentinean heavy metal in these 33–35 polemic years of history? I say 'polemic' because the origin myth, beginning in the days of *Ruedas de Metal* or *Luchando por el Metal*, has always obsessed the specialized press and those discussions that flow throughout the concert space. Whatever path we take, metal is at once a dilemma and an illness. How much has there been written then? A lot, and most of it poorly.

When Gito Minore made his imperative appeal, back in October 2013, to organize the first Heavy Metal Book Fair of Buenos Aires (Centro Cultural La Imaginería – Boedo), a space for discussion was born in which we could discuss the nature of heavy metal as a cultural phenomenon and as a physically locatable reality comprised of magazines, fanzines, performances, bands, collectives, etc. Those of us who could territorially contribute to its edification were present. The Fair was our origin myth as a group, as a writing and educational team, for several reasons. First, those of us who gravitated around GIIHMA (the acronym was yet to come to life) saw ourselves as laborers (mainly belonging to the realm of education). This class attribute becomes indispensable to understanding one particular verse: 'por sentimiento, locura y pasión / Se nos ve de negros vestidos'[1] ('Aguante Bonavena', Almafuerte, 1999). Identity superseded the triviality or the symbolic meaning of a color, an attire, a mere anthropological souvenir, instead cementing an apparatus of identification, of belonging, of a more defined power, with a significant history. We form an active part of our country's working class, like the composers and artists that nourished our childhood.

Second, inquiring and exploring in detail the vast work of specialized metal journalism we came to the conclusion that Wikipedia can already cover, replace, indulge, and award them. With a few honorable exceptions, such as César Fuentes Rodríguez, we found nothing more than a music lover's historicist eagerness: sheer descriptivism, empty of any worth, nothing that orality could not replace. In that space, we encountered that which the university exploits: vacancy. If there is a reading culture or an audience, its visualization must be imminent. In and around the fairs, the cinema debate clubs, the open classes, and the street corners – the highly cherished street corner: hermetic, cryptic, and epistemic – the same questions were being asked. Questions that inquired about a subject (as Gito Minore taught us) of investigation, not an object, with its uncritical and unreal quotidian distance. We are putting our necks at stake here.

Third, if the works that came to us from the academy followed the repressive protocol of the 'subject up to this point' and the subordination of heavy metal as a simple methodology (an art of signatures), we had to work to get past the masturbatory tendencies of scientific solipsism. The effect of high-brow scientific pretentiousness contained in papers and monographs disgusts us. Without abnegating our thorough transit through the university, our experiences as students and educators, we – morally – had to purge our written and oral output of all academic prestige and of all the childish vanity of the Academy. In this sense, GIIHMA[2] recovers the great ('the best of national heavy metal', Iorio would say with the lyric's proper arbitrariness and despotism) yet now mostly inexistent, tradition of Argentinean essay writing, a tradition we had to recover by force. That is why Cultura Metálica I y II came to be (Clara Beter Ediciones); that is why we offered a seminar open to the public and free of charge in April 2015; that is why we actively participate in congresses, conferences, in radio and in graphic media (Andén and Marcha – https://www.andendigital.com.ar) advocating these words; that is why we keep exploring through our writing and not through a survey of dates. We do not deny our passing through the university – we have gone through it laboring – because between its many hallways we *crisscrossed* each other. We allowed ourselves to say that their ways of grasping writing were not our own, period. The discussion is in depth, it is profound, and it interpellates us. Which readings, which knowledge, which subjects flow through the materiality of national heavy metal? Is there a territorial inflection?; an Argentinean 'language' of metal music? Evidently, the answer is yes, or at least that is how we imagine it. Because the terror-laden jaws of the essay form, as a platform for discussion, are, ultimately, the only ones that possess the necessary traits that will allow us to traverse the multidimensionality of Argentinean heavy metal. How do we avoid the nationalistic poetics and politics explicit in its lyrics, in its audiovisual artifacts, in its melodies? And if politics are present, is there, inevitably, an imaginary representation of them? Only an interdisciplinary team could bring forth this approach; this book is proof of that. Because we envisioned ourselves as a fist, GIIHMA could dialectically overcome the barriers set up by the disciplinary fields and their fascist languages, as Roland Barthes has taught us. Only after understanding that the present is urgent and

Argentinean heavy metal intervenes with it, could we come to see ourselves within a tradition characterized by struggle. Because popular culture and its supporters have omitted or ridiculed us, we repaid them with their worst fate: everyday there are more of us … dressed in black. Larralde[3] was right: religion is located here.

We would like to express our deep and fraternal gratitude to Sandra Gasparini, Oscar Blanco, Susana Cella, César Fuentes Rodríguez (and the Tiempos Violentos family), Fabiana Roth, Miguel Ángel Oropeza, Gustavo Zavala, Alejandro Taranto, Revista Efecto Metal, Periódico Andén, Portal de Noticias Marcha, Alicia Miño, Tachas hasta en la sopa, El Club de los Intolerantes, Centro Cultural El Umbral and ESTA magazine (Audiovisual Commission of CEFyL, Facultad de Filosofía y Letras, UBA), Santiago Pogonza (Enfermo Metal), Gabriel Colombus, Brandy con caramelos, *Rock y Freud* (Conexión abierto, Radio *UAI*), Santiago 'Gallo' Bluquermann y Javier 'Kanario' Compiano (Vórterix), Juan Di Natale, Difusión Parlante, Contragolpe (Frecuencia Zero), Corriendo La Voz, Sigmus Desconocidos, Monoambiente (Nacional Rock), Barricada TV, Clara Sirvén (Radio UBA), WYWH.COM.AR, Pablo Díaz Marenghi, Fernando Ferro (Revista La Vereda), Daniel Gigena, Andrés Miguel Alcaraz, Daniel Gigena, Joaquín Amat, Dani Avellaneda, La Mejor Arma, and the names go on … for supporting and disseminating our work.

We extend a special thanks and affirm our undying support to the White Duke (Javier Andrés Moreno Iglesias) who generously opened up his space for us at Mar del Plata (Nevermind), and who in recent times has been assaulted violently and cowardly by fascists backed by local politics.

We shall never forget the unconditional support of the wonderful folks who took the class 'Averting the weakening: An approximation to Argentinean heavy metal as an object of intersections' at the Facultad de Filosofía y Letras (UBA). This book is dedicated to you.

NOTES

1. 'because of feelings, madness and passion/In black we are seen' (t/n).
2. Acronym for Grupo de Investigación Interdisciplinaria sobre el Heavy Metal Argentino (Group for Interdisciplinary Research on Argentinian Heavy Metal) (t/n).
3. José Larralde is a contemporary Argentine poet, singer and songwriter of vast trajectory and recognition, rooted in the traditional Argentinean genres such as the *milonga campera*. He has had a fundamental influence on the work of Ricardo Iorio.

Translator's Note

Juan Manuel López Baio

Translating these pages has been a challenging task, for within them the authors have made the remarkable effort of thinking in the crevices and in the margins, formulating a reflection that was yet to be imagined, envisioned, and spoken. At the core: Argentinean heavy metal. Not its history (though we will find in the book a great deal of historical information, indeed necessary for achieving their goal), but its *singularity*. And, as Roland Barthes says (it is not by chance that he is one of the recurring authors cited in the book), 'to the precision of the target corresponds a waver of the name'.

The complex and intricate nature of the original material with which I worked, resulted in the translation before you. And it is because Argentinean heavy metal is indeed a most singular expression, that I have had to make some decisions in order to convey this singularity so carefully outlined by the authors.

Argentinean heavy metal resonates with the echoes of its British linage, and yet it is fully and thoroughly transformed by our own idiosyncrasies. The decision to take a foreign genre and appropriate it was made at the point of origin, as the genre laid its cornerstone: the bands that started up the movement chose to write and sing, not just in Spanish, but in *argentino*. Thus, the lyrics have been imprinted from the beginning with traces of our own origins: *gauchesque* literature, *lunfardo* argot, and the most contemporary city slang merge to produce a unique voice. Many of the resulting expressions produced by this voice have no equivalent in English, direct or indirect, for they refer to experiences, feelings, themes, and nuances that are immanent to our own historical becoming. I dealt with these situations using different approaches.

In many cases, I have looked for the closest equivalent and made footnotes expanding and explaining further connotations, referring to facts and figures that would at least suggest the full intended sense. In other cases, I have taken some liberties in the use of English neologisms or ad hoc expressions that, though uncommon, would be legible, and which, alongside the corresponding notes, would hopefully reflect the meaning with more precision and subtleness. Finally, some words or expressions I chose to leave in *argentino*, explaining their meaning below and permitting the original form to pierce through with its foreign presence in the English text, transmitting the full force of its sound.

Whatever the case may be, the reader who wants to take a deep dive in the heavy waters of Argentinean heavy metal should take these notes as a hitchhiker's, or better yet, a motorcyclist's guide: names in a map that invite a full-throttle journey. The songs, the artists, the history, the music, the lyrics, are all out there, immediately accessible through innumerable websites on the Internet. *Read while you listen. Listen while you read.* Experience the whole thing, and *bang your head to it.* Then, you *will* understand.

Furthermore, the GIIHMA is an active group of fierce people, alive and kicking, that will happily respond to the call of metal heads around the world who want to know more about and understand better what is going on here, at the South of the South of the world. The arm is stretched out, and the hand is open, so: *come you all, here is a place next to the metal brigade.*

Introduction: A Window into Heavy Metal Scholarship in the Global South

Nelson Varas-Díaz, Daniel Nevárez Araujo, and

Emiliano Scaricaciottoli

Tengo en las venas una sangre y una queja que está latente y no es azul
Tengo en mis venas sangre fuerte metalera/Y una esperanza, la del sur.

('Venas de Acero', Tren Loco 2008)

Introducing this book to readers like you calls for a different approach. Editors usually concentrate on the contents of the book, highlight particular chapters, and describe its overall contributions to a field of knowledge. Doing so in this manner, and for this particular book, feels like a disservice to the underlying story that gave birth to this body of work. In this case, we feel a distinctive approach is needed because the story of how this book came into existence and what it could mean for those who were unaware of its initial publication, hopefully until now, are probably just as important as its content. Therefore, with the leniency of the readers, we wish to take a different path in this introductory note. We will do so by concentrating on the group of authors that brought this work to bear, the context in which it was developed, and what we feel it means to heavy metal music scholarship.

Let us begin with the authors of the book, or rather, the collective of individuals that have brought it to light. The chapters in this book were written by members of the Grupo de Investigación Interdisciplinaria sobre el Heavy Metal Argentino (GIIHMA), or the Group for Interdisciplinary Research on Argentinian Heavy Metal. The GIIHMA is a collective of metal fans, scholars, and activists who have engaged in a joint effort to reflect on the development and permanence of heavy metal culture in their particular country. Their endeavor is specifically important for several reasons. First, they are one of the first scholarly collectives to engage in heavy metal related scholarship in South America. This fact alone is important, as research on heavy metal music has met resistance in many academic settings in the Latin American region. Therefore, it is not coincidental that the GIIHMA has engaged with, but remained strategically distanced from, traditional academic settings. They usually present their work in non-traditional book fairs and scenarios associated with Argentina's working class.

Second, the GIIHMA has shattered the idea of the lone-wolf scholar who engages in research as a solitary process. They have decided to participate in their research endeavor in a *collectivist* manner, holding regular meetings, releasing position statements as a group entity, and refusing to appear in public activities as individual authors, but rather as a research community. This communal approach toward metal scholarship distances itself from many endeavors in North America and Europe, where the idea of the lonely scholar still permeates metal research and holds a certain level of allure.

Third, the GIIHMA has never lost sight of the social and political implications of heavy metal music in their country. Far from echoing the call to distance metal from politics, so frequently heard in the global north, they echo the working class voices that marked early post-dictatorship metal music in Argentina and directly engage in political reflections. They have released position statements on issues related to homophobia, sexism, and the oppression of the working class, among many other social matters. This endeavor, as one might expect, has garnered them as many supporters as detractors. The GIIHMA has even gone so far as to call out important, and sometimes seemingly untouchable, figures in Argentina's metal scene over what they understand to be racist and xenophobic positions. In summary, presenting this book without understanding the group that developed it would be a chimera; it would deprive it of its context, and therefore render it meaningless.

Another crucial factor that must be described in order to better understand the importance of this book is its context, specifically, some general characteristics of Argentina's metal scene. Of course, we (Daniel and Nelson) describe this context from the perspective of outsiders, which in this case we understand is a great benefit as it allows us to explain how that scene is perceived from outside the country. Although some of our research has allowed us to know the scene from the inside (Varas-Díaz, Rivera-Segarra and Nevárez 2019), this dual positioning helps us place the book in its context.

Argentina's metal scene has always been ahead of its time. Take, for example, the release of the album entitled *Luchando por el Metal* (Fighting for Metal) by legendary local band V8. The album was released in 1983, the same year Metallica released their album *Kill em' All* in the United States. Although we feel somewhat uneasy with this comparison as it positions a band in the global north as the standard to follow, we are also aware of the impact this album had in the metal community in that particular year. Argentina had its own important release that year in parallel with what would become the genre's most commercially successful band. Few people seem to put these two facts together, but when it is done, it speaks to how advanced Argentina's metal scene was at the time. Although the global north would become familiar with Latin American metal music mostly through Sepultura's album *Beneath the Remains* in 1989, bands like V8 were ahead of the game. They had created a locally influential album even before the Brazilians had released the albums *Morbid Visions* in 1986 or *Schizophrenia* in 1987. In summary, while the world was becoming familiar with Latin American metal through the lens of Brazil, Argentinians already had their local heroes.

The Argentinian scene, while being ahead of its time, seemed to be self-contained. Some of its most important artists have rarely left Argentina, or have simply toured in neighboring countries. Seminal bands like Almafuerte would still be large draws in the local concert circuit despite never playing on US or European soil. This characteristic, which could be explained by the massive geographical distance from metal epicenters worldwide, would yield a self-contained scene with a rabid fan base in which music and Argentinian nationalism would seamlessly mingle. Although the Argentinian scene would remain a relative secret for the metal industry in the global north, the experience would be very different for its neighboring countries in the global south, particularly Latin America. Any scholar, or metal fan for that matter, who has traveled through the region will attest to the respect the Argentinian scene has in Latin America due to its longevity and the number of active bands.

The two themes described above, the book's authors and the characteristics of the local metal scene under study, set this book apart from other scholarly endeavors in metal music studies. It has been developed in a collective manner and through constant group discussion, thus challenging traditional academic work based on the singular opinions of authors or less-than-dialogically edited collections. It is also written from the perspective of authors who see metal as a genre beyond entertainment, helping readers understand its potential for social change. Finally, since it is written about a metal scene that is mostly ignored by metal scholarship and the international music industry, it opens a window into what metal does in one corner of the global south. These issues, even if sometimes inadvertent, serve as an important challenge to metal scholarship in the global north.

The Global South Blind Spot in Metal Studies

Research on heavy metal in the global south has increased exponentially in the past decade. Published articles and books about metal scenes in places like Nepal (Green 2012), Israel (Kahn-Harris 2012), Japan (Kawano and Hosokawa 2012), Malta (Bell 2012), Turkey (Hecker 2012), South Africa (Hoad 2014), Egypt (LeVine 2008), Puerto Rico (Varas-Díaz, Mendoza, Rivera, and González 2016), Cuba (Varas-Díaz, González-Sepúlveda, and Rivera Amador 2018), the Dominican Republic (Mendoza, Varas-Díaz, Rivera-Segarra and Vélez 2018), and Brazil (Dos Santos Silva 2018) evidence that metal is a global phenomenon (Jeremy Wallach, Berger and Greene 2012) and scholars have taken notice. Still, blind spots continue to show that some areas of the world have received more attention than others. Latin America, for example, has remained ignored in book collections that have aimed to propose a global approach to the musical genre, neglecting to include the region in a representative manner (Turner 2018). We understand this omission happens due to several reasons.

One of the main reasons for the omission of Latin America in metal music studies is language. The scholarly work being developed in the region has been published mostly in Spanish or Portuguese as it emerges from theses and dissertations carried out by young students as part of their higher education studies. These efforts are developed in their native languages and, when published in regional journals, fail to make their entrance into the scholarly databases and conference discussions in which metal scholarship is mostly consumed, specifically, the United States and Europe. Unfortunately, academic journals in which metal scholarship is published in the global north and the conferences in which it is discussed have done little to address this language gap and remain focused on English as the main language of exchange. A notable exception has been a special issue on Latin America metal published in the journal *Metal Music Studies* from UK publishing company Intellect. The issue was edited by Claudia Azevedo, Daniel Nevárez and myself, and included articles in Spanish and Portuguese, accompanied by their English translations (Varas-Díaz, Azevedo, and Nevárez 2018). This book, originally published in Spanish, later translated by Juan Manuel López Baio, and now fully revised and edited by us, is another effort to address this language gap.

A second reason for the omission of Latin America in metal music studies is of an economic nature; we are, of course, speaking specifically about poverty. Many of the students and scholars that engage in research in the region do so despite an extreme lack of funding for their endeavors. This becomes further complicated when their research reaches a stage of dissemination, which usually happens through academic conferences. These events are almost exclusively held in the global north and the implications of travel for these emerging scholars are nefarious. The exchange rate between their local currency and that of the US dollar or the Euro, to take two examples, make it almost impossible for them to take part in these events. Thus, research findings remain limited to small local events and have a hard time reaching a global audience. Therefore, they are rarely cited in the metal literature of the global north, and thus, render these efforts almost inexistent for other scholars.

These two issues, the use of local language and lack of economic resources, seem to foster the existing blind spot toward metal scholarship in the global south and Latin America in particular. Nevertheless, they must be understood as part of a larger problem ailing research on a global scale, specifically, academic imperialism. This position fosters the notion, sometimes explicitly and at other times tacitly, that knowledge production is limited to the global north and its university-affiliated individuals. Therefore, it is mostly shared and consumed in the global north. Take for example the biannual conferences of the International Society for Metal Studies (ISMMS), of which both Daniel and I are members. The first four conferences, arguably the most important events for metal scholarship in the world, have all taken place in the United States and Europe. ISMMS' 2021 conference will take place in Mexico, after a growing number of scholars from the region have slowly influenced the decision-making process within the organization. These decisions are frequently implemented without malice or an explicit desire to silence research in the global south. Still, these practices can sometimes amount to academic imperialism and the tacit devaluation of knowledge produced in the global south. It is a great boon that organizations like ISMMS are willing to shift gears and engage the global south.

This edited collection is a concrete effort to address the two issues described above. Its initial publication was made in Spanish by a local publishing house with scarce resources for promotion. This guaranteed that the book would be distributed mostly by word of mouth, and its impact outside Argentina was extremely limited due to the high cost of shipping within Latin America. These costs were even higher, and almost inaccessible, when considering shipping to the United States and Europe. Emiliano Scaricaciottoli, who edited the Spanish version of the book, had procured an initial translation of the material and contacted us to discuss its potential publication. We then proceeded to establish a publishing agreement with Intellect in the United Kingdom, revised and adapted the initial translation, and reedited the book in its entirety. Therefore, the final product is a collaboration between scholars in the global south and the global north (although it warrants mentioning that Daniel and Nelson have lived in the global south most of their lives), via a translation that is sensitive to the nuances of the message the GIIHMA originally wished to transmit in Spanish, and released by a publisher like Intellect whose team is aware of the need to disseminate research from diverse regions of the world, and continues to actively do so.

The Contributions in This Book

Taken together, the chapters in this book paint an initial picture of metal in Argentina – its birth, its growth, its meaning, and its use as a tool of an otherwise invisible segment of Argentinean society. The picture is one of struggle, oppression, and insurmountable odds; but it is also one of perseverance, camaraderie, and hope. Each chapter touches on either a moment, an influential figure, or a particular dominant tendency within the field and/or practice of metal. And while each has its own flavor or methodology, the reader will soon note that they also seek to speak to each other, be it through direct or indirect conversation.

Gustavo Torreiro sets the tone for the book in Chapter 1, grounding the study of metal in Argentina on one key question: can heavy metal be seen as a subculture, not only within the country at large, but within the rock and popular music genres themselves? Torreiro's approach helps define the identities that have circulated and continue to circulate around metal, particularly within the context of a country that experienced a dictatorship during the 1970s and 1980s, only to later adopt a neoliberal democratic model born out of that same dictatorship. Thus, for Torreiro, metal in Argentina is to be seen as a working class movement whose members coalesce around a shared identity based on the need to push back against the dominant ideological classes, both then and now.

By deploying the Bourdieusian concept of 'field' to the study of heavy metal, Luciano Scarrone calls attention in Chapter 2 to the treacherous relationship between the margins metal expects and intends to inhabit and the markets which seek to absorb the genre for consumption. The field of heavy metal exhibits many of the complexities and contradictions found in neoliberalism and transnationalism, though through heavy metal's countercultural position, these complexities and contradictions become even more amplified, particularly in Argentina. Scarrone calls attention to the way these opposing forces influence each other; however, as he notes, heavy metal (and its followers) represents a force that has found a way (through the use of tools like radio and print publications) to co-opt the market toward its own interests.

In 1986, V8, the influential Argentinian metal band, would release *El Fin de los Inicuos*, their last and most controversial album. The album captures the tension between the band's members (some of whom had recently adopted Evangelicalism), their Argentinian context, and metal music. Tracing a history of white metal (i.e., Christian metal) in Chapter 3, Gito Minore studies the history of

North American Evangelicalism and its deployment as a tool toward the destabilization of the Catholic Church's 'liberation theology' in South America during the 1980s. Additionally, the author sheds some light on the irreconcilable differences between Alberto Zamarbide and Miguel Roldan's Evangelicalism and Ricardo Iorio's adoption of the Basilio Scientific School. Minore is interested in fleshing out these differences, which made white metal's incursion into Argentina fail and V8's adoption of the genre ineffective, ultimately causing the disintegration of Argentinian metal's seminal band.

Chapter 4 is the first to focus solely on the towering figure of Ricardo Iorio. Manuel Bernal and Diego Caballero devote their chapter to analyzing Iorio's post-V8 poetics. More to the point, they are interested in the artist's constant return to the notion of the 'journey' as a guiding principle in his songwriting and his life philosophy during both his Hermética and Almafuerte periods. They argue that for Iorio, the journey takes on different meanings: the need for flight and escape, the call to encounter and make friends, the need to move, the need for self-discovery. In this regard, Iorio represents for the authors a continuation of the *gauchesca* tradition, as they argue that the singer/songwriter taps into the tradition's dominants of the open land, the interior, the authentic, and movement found in the works of artists such as Atahualpa Yupanqui and José Hernández, to name a few.

Juan Ignacio Pisano continues the analysis of Iorio's poetics in Chapter 5. Like Bernal and Caballero, Pisano will find links between Iorio's output and the *gauchesca* tradition. This connection takes place mostly at the level of territoriality, with Iorio seeking to move from the urban to the rural. However, Pisano adds a political and ethical dimension in his analysis, noting how this physical movement brings with it another, more problematic movement: from the rebellious attitude of metal to a nationalist bent of *gauchesca*. Thus, Pisano offers the reader a genealogical study of Iorio's move toward conservatism as evinced in his ever-morphing yet equally constant lyrical output.

Taking Susan Sontag's conception of illness as a discursive construct, Ezequiel Alasia proposes that Argentinian heavy metal's purpose is to reveal the ills of society to its adepts, thus serving as an alternative cure that seeks to rid them of illness by bringing the latter to light. By analyzing lyrics from V8, Hermética, and Almafuerte, among others, Chapter 6 walks the reader through the ways in which illness factors into the work of these bands (all of which have Iorio as their backbone), in the process proposing heavy metal as a mode of resistance. According to Alasia, Argentinian metal achieves this through the foregrounding of language that is class conscious.

Finally, Emiliano Scaricaciottoli surveys the events of December 2001 and the crisis that ensued[1] through the lyrical output that followed. Using semantics as his initial prism, Scaricaciottoli pays close attention to the referential codes deployed within metal songs. While the era's songs contain both abstract and referential strategies, he argues that the period is characterized by an increase in the latter. The author notes how many post-2001 songs from bands like Tren Loco, Horcas, and, of course, Almafuerte (to name a few) use language allusive to the events, identity, and class dynamics as a way to rally the working and lower classes. The result is music that positions itself in a multitude of spaces, both physical and philosophical, thus, demanding a *trans*disciplinary approach to better understand the events and the resultant cultural artifacts.

A Wider Contribution to Metal Music Studies

Although each of the chapters described above makes an important individual contribution to the advancement of heavy metal related scholarship in the global south, we understand that it is their collective agenda which sets them apart from previous work in Argentina, and the region as a whole. First, the collection stresses the importance of understanding heavy metal music in Argentina as southern culture. Its nuances, practices, and particularities evidence how the musical genre does more than reflect local culture and becomes a culture unto itself. Still, metal is part of Argentinian culture, even though local social elites, including academia, might have a hard time accepting this proposal. Second, the chapters shed light on the political dimensions of heavy metal music in Argentina, challenging the apolitical characterization of metal done in the global north (Scott 2012). The GIIHMA has allowed us to venture into a context in which metal music is, and can continue to be, a catalyst for social change and thus aligns itself with other musical genres concerned with social justice. Finally, the book, now in its English version and finally accessible to the global north, serves as a stark reminder of the need to continue challenging traditional ways of producing knowledge in which contributions from the global south are devalued and seen as less profound or scholarly. We hope you enjoy the book, consider it as a reference in your future research, and continue to meditate on the importance of understanding heavy metal music in the global south. There is more out there, and we hope you will be motivated to seek it out.

REFERENCES

Bell, Albert (2012), 'Metal in a micro island state: An insider's perspective', in J. Wallach, H. Berger, and P. Greene (eds), *Metal Rules the Globe*, North Carolina: Duke University Press, pp. 271–93.

Dos Santos Silva, Melina Aparecida (2018), 'Letters, cassette tapes and zines: The circulation of Brazilian heavy metal as a gift system', *Metal Music Studies*, 4:1, pp. 241–49.

Green, Paul (2012), 'Electronic and affective overdrive: Tropes of transgression in Nepal's heavy metal scene', in J. Wallach, H. Berger, and P. Greene (eds.), *Metal Rules the Globe,* North Carolina: Duke University Press, pp. 109–34.

Hecker, Pierre (2012), *Turkish Metal: Music, Meaning, and Morality in a Muslim Society*, New York: Ashgate Pub Co.

Hoad, Catherine (2014), '"Ons is saam"': Afrikaans metal and rebuilding whiteness in the Rainbow Nation', *International Journal of Community Music*, 7:2, pp. 189–204.

Kahn-Harris, Keith (2012), 'You are from Israel and that is enough to hate you forever: Racism, globalization, and play within the global extreme metal scene', in J. Wallach, H. Berger, and P. Greene (eds), *Metal Rules the Globe*, North Carolina: Duke University Press, pp. 200–26.

Kawano, Kei and Hosokawa, Shuhei (2012), 'Thunder in the far east: The heavy metal industry in 1990s Japan', in J. Wallach, H. Berger, and P. Greene (eds), *Metal Rules the Globe*, North Carolina: Duke University Press, pp. 247–70.

LeVine, Mark (2008), *Heavy Metal Islam: Rock, Resistance, and the Struggle for the Soul of Islam*, New York: Three Rivers Press.

Mendoza, Souhail, Varas-Díaz, Nelson, Rivera-Segarra, Eliut, and Vélez, Carlos (2018), 'Media representations of metal music in the Dominican Republic: Between oppression and social resistance', *Metal Music Studies*, 4:1, pp. 197–208.

Scott, Niall (2012), 'Heavy metal and the deafening threat of the apolitical', *Popular Music History*, 6:1, pp. 224–39.

Turner, Joe (2018), 'Review of the books *Global Metal Music and Culture: Current Directions in Metal Studies* and *Connecting Metal to Culture: Unity in Disparity*', *Popular Music*, 37:3, pp. 509–12.

Varas-Díaz, Nelson, Azevedo, Claudia, and Nevárez, Daniel (2018), 'Metal in Latin America', *Metal Music Studies*, 4:1, pp. 131–35.

Varas-Díaz, Nelson, González-Sepúlveda, Osvaldo, and Rivera Amador, Andrés (2018), 'From the "patio" to the "agency": The emergence and structuring of metal music in revolutionary Cuba', *Metal Music Studies*, 4:1, pp. 137–46.

Varas-Díaz, Nelson, Mendoza, Sigrid, Rivera, Eliut, and González, Osvaldo (2016), 'Metal at the fringe: A historical perspective on Puerto Rico's underground metal scene', in B. Gardenour Walter, G. Riches, D. Snell, and B. Bardine (eds), *Heavy Metal Studies and Popular Culture*, England: Palgrave Macmillan, pp. 99–120.

Varas-Díaz, Nelson, Rivera-Segarra, Eliut, and Nevárez, Daniel (2019), 'Coloniality and resistance in Latin American metal music: Death as experience and strategy', *Hispanic Issues Online*, 23, pp. 226–51.

Wallach, Jeremy, Berger, Harris, and Greene, Paul (2012), *Metal Rules the Globe: Heavy Metal Music Around the World*, Durham, NC: Duke University Press.

NOTE

1. Starting in December 2001, a throng of Argentineans would hit the streets to protest Fernando de la Rúa's government and its adoption of austerity measures at the behest of the IMF. During the crisis, Argentina would experience violent riots, with many civilians dying at the hands of law enforcement due to the latter's unscrupulous use of lethal force. The crisis would eventually result in de la Rúa's resignation and a period of economic, political, social instability.

1

Heavy Metal as a Subculture in Argentina: Identity and Resistance

Gustavo Torreiro

Heavy metal appeared suddenly in Argentina at the beginning of the 1980s, within a particular political and historical climate during which the nation found itself under the rule of a military dictatorship that had begun in 1976. Despite lacking the strength of its earlier years, the dictatorship continued to dominate the Argentinean political and social scene of the time.

The incursion of heavy metal as a cultural[1] phenomenon into Argentina does not seem to be a random event. The following chapter seeks to respond to the many questions surrounding the irruption of this cultural movement into the country and the ways in which it has manifested itself. To begin, we will analyze whether it is possible to approach heavy metal in Argentina as a subculture[2] while also considering the type of identity such a genre assumes within the nation. Second, we will consider whether there are elements that allow for the consideration of heavy metal as a movement that originates from the poor and working classes, emerging as a way for these classes to resist the dominant class ideology. This chapter will also look at how heavy metal opposed the dominant ideology of a period that spanned from its origins in the 1980s – with the rise of the first noteworthy bands (Riff and V8) – to the end of the 1990s. With this final objective in mind, we will develop and delineate a timeline of this period. The first period to be analyzed takes place during the military dictatorship (1976–83). Here, we will take a closer look at the content within and the reasoning behind many of the heavy metal lyrics that openly confront the dictatorship. Following this analysis, we will look at the period when democracy returns to Argentina (1983–89). Finally, we will consider the era of resistance born during the 1990s. In this period the neoliberal politics, partially implemented during the dictatorship, fully mature under the presidency of Carlos Menem.

The issue of class will not take a secondary position in this analysis. Taking this into account, and following Louis Althusser's work and his analyses of society as a structure defined by class struggle, this chapter will consider the position this cultural movement occupies in Argentina as it pertains to said struggle. Althusser asserts that culture forms part of what he calls the ideological state apparatuses (ISAs). ISAs are intricately related to those classes that possess the means of production and which, consequently, control state institutions. However, precisely because they are marked by their connection to ideology, it is possible to understand

> their capacity to not only be objects of the class struggle, but spaces where said class struggle takes place, often in highly contentious ways. The powerful upper classes (or class alliances) cannot enforce their laws on the ISAs as easily as they do when it comes to the (repressive) state apparatus.
>
> (Althusser 2005: 28)

It is the possibility of a contentious class struggle[3] within the ISAs that gives the exploited classes the means to resist the dominant ideology.

Subculture and Identity

If we can think of heavy metal in Argentina as a subculture, it is because it originates as a subset of a 'parent culture'[4] defined by its class composition. A central argument of this chapter is that the social subject to whom heavy metal lyrics allude to, specifically in Argentina, and which enables us to consider this movement as a subculture that arises from the subordinate classes is characterized by one of two identities. Either this subject is a member of a working class that is suffering and resisting the onslaughts of neoliberal policies which were first enforced during the Military Dictatorship of 1976/83,[5] or the subject belongs to a lower class that has already lost the 'privileges' of belonging to the working class as a consequence of the disintegration of the labor world, a disintegration precipitated by the imposition of neoliberalism in 1976: 'Poor people clamor for a crust of bread/The rich have become their executioners' ('La Mano Maldita', *Un Paso más en la Batalla*, V8 1985).

The lyrics of Hermética's song 'Gil Trabajador', a song that offers a working-class critique against the vision of a society increasingly dominated by a neoliberal culture that undervalues hard work, will be taken as emblematic of this subculture's relationship with the working class: 'With my meager salary/I cannot avoid/the bitter taste of this bad moment/while the world, the police and a thief/dub me, in mockery, the simpleton[6] worker' ('Gil Trabajador', *Ácido Argentino*, Hermética 1991). The lyrics enact, through their criticism of society, a reclaiming of the traditional values of the working class, which, in the specific context being analyzed, have been disputed by the dominant ideology the subculture is challenging.

It is worth mentioning the analysis made by Maristella Svampa (2000) who, in studying the identity of metal workers, introduces as a sample case the testimony of Roque, a worker from the metal industry who identifies himself as a metalhead. Svampa states that Roque 'is excluded from the middle class by a position and a function in the social structure ("I get up at four in the morning to go to work") but also by the recreational spaces he frequents ("I don't visit nightclubs as they do, those that have a little more money than me") and the clothing he wears, among others'. On the other hand, Roque still voices the pride he feels at being a metal worker: 'I always loved the sight of scrap and sheet metal bundles'[7] (2000: 131). We would argue that the convergent identities of metalhead and lower-class laborer found in Roque can also be found to coexist in the heavy metal subculture of Argentina. The heavy metal subculture is formed around the subordinate classes; as a result, the subculture distinguishes itself from the rest of society through the position occupied by its members within the social structure as well as through the subjectivity or identification markers the movement acquires.

In order to closely analyze the identity that forms around the genre in Argentina, we will deploy Stuart Hall's definition of identity. Hall affirms that

> identities are born from difference, not at the margins of that difference. This implies the radically disturbing acknowledgment that the 'positive' meaning of any given term – and with it its 'identity' – can only be discovered through its relationship with the Other, the relationship with that which it is not, with that which it precisely lacks, with that which it has denominated as its constitutive exterior.
>
> (2010: 18)

From this perspective, we can think of the metalhead identity in Argentina as an opposition or as a limit to dominant culture, as that which the latter is not. Thus, we can account for a constitutive exterior that draws a line between what it is to be a metalhead and what it is not. And that exterior is not defined solely by the sound of the music those belonging to the subculture listen to or the common traits shared by those found within the subculture; the identity is also determined, in great measure, by the limit, the rejection, the resistance to the dominant culture. We can see this opposition to dominant culture in the work of a band like Riff, who voice their rejection of the modernity that was drawing near; 'consequently, Riff's metal style – with its aggressively gothic and futurist horror components – proposes a subjectivity which implies a contrarian identity, an identity that rails against what it sees as an imposed system, the new modern city' (Blanco and Scaricaciottoli 2014: 105).

In its lyrics, Riff attacks modern values and trends that invade and modify the city. An opposition between modernity and the values that characterize the heavy metal subculture can be traced in different songs, as is the case in a song titled 'Maquinación': 'Today we decide to reclaim/a trace of our identity/ on the road lies/your uneventful modernity' ('Maquinación', *Contenidos*, Riff 1982). We can think of this opposition to modernity as functioning in two distinct manners: on the one hand, it offers itself as a resistance against the rise of a new way of producing and consuming promoted by neoliberal policies that invade, not just the cities, but society at large; on the other hand, it is an attack on modern groups and bands that appeared on the Argentinean rock and pop scene during the 1980s. Returning to the oppositions expressed during the identification processes, it can be argued that the values of modernity stand as an important antithetical element. In other words, and to be as clear as possible: it is not possible to be modern and belong to the heavy metal subculture at the same time.

Whereas the values of modernity represent a fundamental antagonist in the music of Riff, in the music of a band like V8, the position of the antagonist is taken up by the pacifism found in the figure of the hippie: 'Those sick of withstanding/ the weeping of the peacemongers/those fed up with seeing/the faces that recall yesteryears/join us, there is a place/in this metal brigade/deranged people who are not like/our inland hippiedom' ('Brigadas Metálicas', *Luchando por el Metal*, V8 1983). The metal brigades, the metalheads, cannot be subjects who, recalling the repression suffered by the lower classes under the civic–military dictatorship, willingly accept some form of complacent pacifism. Violent struggle surfaces as a response to a system and a political context that has historically attacked the subordinate classes. To allude to 'our inland hippiedom' is to draw 'a line dividing what came to be known as *national rock* from the heavy metal output of bands like V8 who, tapping into the furor and the anger of the moment, reclaimed what had been abandoned in rock, that is, its imperative to protest' (Blanco and Scaricaciottoli 2014: 111).

While an extended analysis of this aspect is beyond the purview of this chapter, it is important to mention that a fundamental aspect defining a subculture's identity is its style (clothing, hairstyle, etc.). This style functions, on the one hand, as an identifier that marks off boundaries of belonging, and which, at the same time, ties the subculture to prior subcultures. It also links them to the parent culture, given that it takes elements from both and resignifies them.

Metal's Resistance

When we talk about resisting, we are talking about resisting the dominant ideology from a specific position: that is, from the subordinate or lower classes. As stated earlier, heavy metal in Argentina arises from these classes, and it is from them that a resistance will be developed against the dominant ideology developed within the different historical periods analyzed in this text. Resistance will manifest itself in several ways: first, as a resistance to the dominant culture and the values of the dominant ideology; but also as a resistance to the social and economic policies that the dominant classes, as embodied by current governments, impose and that directly impact the popular classes.

Resistance during the Last Dictatorship

The last civic-military dictatorship, which operated from 1976 to 1983, had a crystal clear objective: to impose a deindustrializing economic plan based on neoliberal policies that specifically harmed the working and lower classes. It must be noted that the implementation of the neoliberal economic plan required the disciplining of those subordinate classes who, prior to the coup d'état, had attained a high degree of organization and consciousness, to the point that they managed to wrestle away some power from the dominant classes, even within the military sphere. In order to dismantle and discipline the organized working and lower classes, a level of repression was enacted that, because of its scale, lacked any precedents in Argentinean history. It is within this context that this cultural movement suddenly appears in Argentina, and it is within this arena that it will interrupt the dominant ideology.

One of the first strong critiques that emerges is levied against the repression felt under the dictatorship. Employing the seemingly innocent device of a visit to the dental office, the song 'Torturador' by V8 playfully winks at the listener as it proceeds to code the dentist as a torturer, depicting the atrocities carried out in clandestine detention centers during those years: 'The molar is already dead/your will succumbs/your desperation/prevents you from confronting/that professional/of buccal torture/of the subtle injection/listen and listen/to his sorrowful version/your dread, your pain' ('Torturador', *Luchando por el Metal*, V8 1983).

Another critique that emerges is hurled at the pacifism that a large part of society adopts in the face of all the repression suffered by the working and lower classes. It is necessary, at this point, to return to the criticisms made toward the hippie, partially highlighted earlier under the 'Subculture and Identity' subheading. The hippie is presented as the stereotype of a particular class (the middle class) that is going to adopt a complacent stance in the face of military repression. In her book about V8, Ana Mourin posits that, when Iorio[8] refers to the hippies, he is referring to,

> bandwagoners who adopt hippiedom as a fashion, ignoring the fact that the primitive energy which generated the birth of the movement on the planet has already been lost, extricating themselves, through the placid inactivity they advocate, from the moment of violent political repression that was being experienced in the country.
>
> (Mourin 1993)

This reading is noteworthy because it offers an interpretation of Iorio's stance, particularly as it pertains to repression and society's inaction and pacifism in front of said repression (a stance that can be extended more widely to heavy metal as a cultural movement). Seen from Iorio's perspective, the State-sponsored repression could not be confronted with pacifism; violence had to be met with violence: 'Stop with the deception/the present is pain/I live in reality/and from her, my reaction comes/For I am tired of the whimpering/that never gave me anything/from being calm/or patient before the repression' ('Momento de luchar', *Un Paso más en la Batalla*, V8 1985). V8's lyrics makes Iorio's critique explicit when it comes to the patience adopted by hippiedom in the context of a repression that struck the lower and working classes.

The Malvinas War will stand as another focal site of critique against the dictatorship on the part of the heavy metal subculture. The Malvinas affair will be taken up in heavy metal lyrics as a national issue. In various lyrics, the conscripted soldier will be elevated to the stature of a hero, officers will be degraded and accused of cowardice, Galtieri[9] will be equated to Margaret Thatcher, and society will be criticized for turning its back on soldiers returning from the Malvinas:

> With Thatcher to one side, a drunk Galtieri on the other
> and the death of soldiers in the south....
> I wanted to take root and build a home
> but now I live with the belligerent death
> between cowardly officers behind
> and honorable soldiers on the front
>
> ('1982', *Endemoniado*, Apocalipsis 1985)

A similar stance can be found in V8's lyrics: 'You rushed to war/for your land and for your people/the ones that have forgotten you/and who still harass your present' ('Deseando Destruir y Matar', *Un Paso más en la Batalla*, V8 1985).

The reclamation of the conscripted soldier can be read in two different, yet complementary ways: on one side, it is the vindication of those who truly fought, put their bodies on the line, and – in many cases – died during the war; on the other side, it stands as an act of identification with that conscripted soldier. It should go without saying that the vast majority of the conscripted soldiers who fought in the Malvinas were youths from the lower and working classes; youths from the same classes from which heavy metal originates.

Democratic Recuperation: Between Hope and Disillusion

The return to democracy inspired great hope, primarily because 'broad sectors of society chose to believe that the principles of an equitable State, principles like the division of powers, the just application of the law by "independent" judges, and the widespread validity of personal and political freedoms, would be sufficient to guarantee a fairer brand of capitalism' (Filadoro et al. 2008: 422); but the working and lower classes were the first to become disillusioned when their suffering continued as a result of the neoliberal policies initially imposed during the dictatorship, and which remained in place under the Alfonsín government.

This disillusionment will be captured in heavy metal lyrics that will also accuse society of adopting escapism and individualism in the face of a democratic model that attacks its working and lower classes through the promotion of harmful economic plans. Society will be portrayed as an 'anesthetized mass' that cannot develop a collective project: 'The great anesthetized mass/wallows in selfishness/ And if it finds any sense/it has surrendered to escapism' ('Masa Anestesiada', *Hermética*, Hermética 1989). Society is asleep while the working classes are 'victims of the purge': 'The city sleeps during the blackout/the purge is taking place/ and lost in the confusion/are the drowned screams of my despair' ('Víctimas del Vaciamiento', *Hermética*, Hermética 1989). There is, on the part of the subculture, an invitation for society at large to awaken, to rise out of the slumber produced by too much anesthesia, and to understand that the 'moment to fight' has arrived. A critique of the values of the modern city and modernity per se are other factors called into question at this point.

Democracy, recently achieved, did not solve the social problems that appeared during the dictatorship. Alfonsín's campaign slogan, which read: 'Democracy feeds, cures and educates', remained just a slogan; words never put into action. The lower and working classes continued to take the brunt of austerity measures imposed by the bourgeoisie, a fact captured in heavy metal lyrics. In the meantime, both the rock and pop scenes practiced their own exclusionary tactics. While not everyone in the rock scene adopted what could be denominated democratic optimism, many bands and albums during those years reflected a self-satisfied enthusiasm, as evinced by the fact that the best-selling album in the country during the 1980s was Miguel Mateos-Zas' *Rockas Vivas*, which contained the hit single 'Tirá, tirá para arriba'.[10] Optimism dominated Argentina's 1980s rock and pop scenes, a fact that speaks of the anesthetized way of life of the middle class. To be fair, though, we must add that punk rock in the 1980s would serve as yet another trench from which another segment would resist the dominant ideology, and that the genre captured the opinions of the lower and working classes.

The 1990s: Neoliberalism and the Social Question

The 1990s, or the 'menemate',[11] we would argue, can be seen as the period in which neoliberal policies consolidated in Argentina. While it is true that a series of economic reforms with a distinct neoliberal slant had been under way since the dictatorship, it is during Menem's presidency that this plan, along with the reforms elaborated by the Washington Consensus, will take root, subsequently transforming the State, the economy, and society in a brutal manner. Restrictive financial policies, liberalization and deregulation of the economy, downsizing of the State, privatization, and a fiscal adjustment plan were the salient points of the decade-long bourgeois plan.

These policies directly impacted the lower and working classes, who in a short span saw their economic and social levels decline. Large-scale unemployment stands as one of the legacies left behind by the decade analyzed here. Continuing its tradition of critique, heavy metal will document this situation through various lyrics: 'The unemployed and low wage laborers of today/Freedom has too high a price/We live amongst the lies and frustration' ('Clase Trabajadora', *¡No me Importa!*, Tren Loco 1996). Disillusionment manifests by way of the people's frustration with a democracy that expresses itself as anti-working class, proceeding with the policies initiated under the civic-military dictatorship. Furthermore, that democracy becomes a 'Swineocracy'[12] in a song by Tren Loco, where all bourgeois institutions are seen as corrupt or anti-working class:

> Swineocracy!
> In the government and the schools
> Swineocracy!
> Police and cocaine
> Swineocracy!
> In the misery, and the repressions
> Swineocracy!

At the frontier and in religions
Swineocracy!
At the workshop and in the office
Swineocracy!
The social climbers and the traitors
Swineocracy!
Labor unions and prisons
Swineocracy!
Goodbye, goodbye my pampas
I leave
I leave for faraway lands
Swineocracy!
('Cerdocracia', *¡No me Importa!*,
Tren Loco 1996)

The disbelief toward a bourgeois democracy does not stop there:

Politicking
a juris doctor
gained support with mere promises
Inviting to a barbecue feast
the people,
who gave their vote trusting
That he possessed social sensibility,
that he would fulfill without yielding
With his campaign speeches,
he weaved his fraud
Mounds of cash he withdrew by plane
where to exactly, nobody knows
Surely they will soon forget him,
and he'll run for office again
('Olvídalo y Volverá por Más',
Víctimas del Vaciamiento, Hermética 1994)

At the heart of metal's critique of the political system, a system that remains deaf to the demands of the working and lower classes, we find a bourgeois democratic system comprised of corrupt politicians who make promises but who ultimately do not fulfill these promises.

Beyond the critique of bourgeois democracy, there exists, in some cases, a vindication of politics as a collective project capable of transforming reality, and an active attitude that calls for resistance against a system that, even within democracy, threatens to annihilate the working and lower classes. This annihilation happens not through the repression and systematic disappearance of people, but through the adoption of economic austerity measures. This combative spirit can be witnessed in the song 'Resistencia' by the group Horcas:

> Unemployment
> lack of food
> falsehood will reign
> To live and grow in misery
> to fight, to die for your existence
> Plague, hunger, and misery
> in isolation the youth will suffer
> between death and torture
> thousands of families condemned they are
> they will live forever
> a harsh betrayal will befall the repressor
> We must resist
> before obscene power
> we must break
> with this system
> resistance, resistance
> ('Resistencia', *Vence*, Horcas 1997)

Resistance presents itself as a political expression and is transformed into a positive and collective action.

The purge during the 1990s was absolute, and the 'victims of the purge' were the lower and working classes who suffered the consequences of the aforementioned policies. Heavy metal, as an expression of the lower and working classes, stood as a form of resistance, in the cultural sphere, against those policies.

Final Thoughts

One basic assumption that guides this chapter is the relationship between heavy metal and the lower and working classes in Argentina. To put it clearly, what this chapter argues is that heavy metal comes out of the subaltern classes and, thus, constitutes itself as a subculture. To assert that this cultural movement emerges from these classes is to hold that class struggle is produced and reproduced within the cultural field.

Taking this perspective into consideration, we have analyzed the relationship between this subculture and the working and lower classes. From this analysis we have delineated the identity of heavy metal in Argentina as a form of resistance, which these classes developed in order to oppose the dominant ideology. At this point it is essential to make the following clarification: to affirm that heavy metal emerges from the lower and working classes is not to say that it gives rise to a classist vision. The heavy metal discourse analyzed through its lyrics acquires different levels of consciousness depending on the historical moment as well as the political vision and the level of class consciousness of each of the authors and bands that were studied. It should be clear that, even though we are studying heavy metal resistance from a general point of view, each of the bands analyzed has a different level of consciousness and there is not one homogeneous or coherent set of beliefs; rather, there is a heterogeneity of critiques and resistances to the system that converge, thanks to a shared heavy metal class identity.

REFERENCES

Almafuerte (1991), *Ácido Argentino*, cassette: Radio Trípoli.

Althusser, Louis (2005), *Ideología y Aparatos Ideológicos de Estado. Freud y Lacan*, Buenos Aires: Editorial Nueva Visión.

Blanco, Oscar and Scaricaciottoli, Emiliano (2014), *Las Letras del Rock en la Argentina: De la Caída de la Dictadura a la Crisis de la Democracia (1983–2001)*, Buenos Aires, Argentina: Colihue.

Feixa, Carles (1999), *De* Jóvenes *Bandas y Tribus: Antropología de la Juventud*, Barcelona: Editorial Ariel.

Filadoro, Ariel, de Luque, Susana, and Giuliani, Alejandra (2008), *Historia Argentina Contemporánea: Pasados Presentes de la Política, la Economía y el Conflicto Social*, Vicente Lopez: Dialektik Editora.

Gramsci, Antonio (2006), *Antología*, Buenos Aires: Editorial Siglo XXI.

Hall, Stuart (2003), *Cuestiones de Identidad Cultural*, Buenos Aires, Argentina: Amorrortu Editores.

Hall, Stuart and Paul du Gay (compilers) (2003), *Cuestiones de Identidad Cultural*, Buenos Aires: Amorrortu.

Hebdige, Dick (2004), *Subcultura: El Significado del Estilo*, Barcelona: Editorial Paidós.

Hermética (1989), *Hermética*, Vinilo: Radio Trípoli.

——— (1994), *Víctimas del Vaciamiento*, cassette: Radio Trípoli.

Horcas (1997), *Vence*, CD: NEMS.

Marx, Karl and Engels, Friedrich (1974), *La Ideología Alemana*, Montevideo, Uruguay: Grijalbo.

——— (2003), *Manifiesto del Partido Comunista*, Buenos Aires: Prometeo Libros.

Mourin, Ana (1993), *V8: Un Sentimiento: Historia de la Banda Precursora del Heavy Metal Argentino*, Buenos Aires: Independent Edition.

Riff (1982), *Contenidos*, Vinilo: Publicaciones Editoriales Americanas.

Svampa, Maristella (2000), 'Identidades astilladas. De la patria metalúrgica al heavy metal', in M. Svampa (ed.), *Desde Abajo. Las Transformaciones de las Identidades Sociales*, Buenos Aires: Biblos, pp. 150–54.

Tren Loco (1996), *¡No me Importa!*, CD: Yugular Records.

V8 (1983), *Luchando por el Metal*, Vinilo: Umbral.

——— (1985), *Un Paso más en la Batalla*, Vinilo, Argentina: Umbral.

NOTES

1. 'We understand the word culture as referring to that level in which social groups develop different life patterns and give expressive form to their social and material life experience. Culture is the mode, the forms, in which groups handle and give expressive form to social and material life experience' (Hall 2003: 69). From this definition it is clear that there are classes that coexist within the same society but, at the same time, those groups or classes differentiate themselves through the relationship they keep with the means of production. It should be noted that 'the class that has at its disposal the means of material production controls, at the same time, the means of spiritual production' (Marx 1974: 50).
2. The term 'subculture' will be understood in the terms defined by Hebdige. Hebdige affirms that subcultures are expressive forms, which ultimately give an account of the fundamental tension between those who occupy power and those who are condemned to subordinate positions and second-class lives. They appear as a form of resistance where contradictions and objections to reigning ideology are expressed. Furthermore, he adds that subcultures arise from subordinate classes, unlike countercultures that are a political project of the middle classes (Hebdige 2004: 180–81).
3. It is necessary to introduce Gramsci's (2006) concept of hegemony as a way to understand class struggle dynamics within the cultural space. The term 'hegemony' alludes to a situation in which a provisional alliance of distinct social groups can exert total social authority. However, Gramsci adds that hegemonic power requires the consent of the dominated majority. It is for this reason that it could never be permanently exerted by the same alliance. Hegemony develops as a movable equilibrium that holds within itself the relations of force within society.
4. The concept of 'parent culture' is taken from Carles Feixa, who affirms that said culture is comprised of 'big cultural networks, fundamentally defined by ethnic and class identities, within which juvenile cultures develop, constituting subsets' (Feixa 1999: 86).
5. 'We are consuming ourselves in this hell/Where injustice and exploitation reign/We are the kind of people that no longer surrender/We live amongst the lies and the frustration' ('Clase Trabajadora', *¡No me Importa!*, Tren Loco 1996).

6. 'gil': Argentinean slang with a heavy suburban accent; it comprises a set of pejorative meanings: gullible, naïve, street-dumb, ignorant, etc.
7. 'chaperío': Argentinean argot that refers to the presence of a messy or untidy set of metal sheets and plates in a metal works workshop or deposit.
8. Ricardo Iorio (Buenos Aires, 1962) is a heavy metal singer and bassist who helped found three of the seminal Argentinian bands in the genre: V8, Hermética, and Almafuerte. Currently, he performs with his solo band, Iorio.
9. Leopoldo Fortunato Galtieri (Caceros, 1926. Buenos Aires, 2006) was an Argentinian general and dictator who stood as the president of Argentina from 1981 to 1982. He was tried in 1985 along with other military chiefs tied to the National Reorganization Process (1976–83). In 1986, he was charged with 'negligence' and sentenced to 12 years in prison for his political and military role in the 1982 Malvinas War (Falklands War). In 1990 he received a pardon from the then president Carlos Saúl Menem; however, new charges were brought against him in 2002 concerning the disappearance of minors during his time as a military commander in the 1970s. He was subsequently placed under house arrest until his death in 2003.
10. Regional expression in which there is a polyvalent use of the Spanish verb 'tirar'. It can be translated both as 'shoot up' or 'pull up'. In both cases the expression is equivalent to 'cheer up' and it denotes the lightweight optimistic attitude pointed to by the author (t/n).
11. I.e. the presidency of Carlos Saúl Menem (1989–99) (t/n).
12. 'Cerdocracia', invented word resulting from the contraction of 'cerdo' (pig/swine) and 'democracia' (democracy). It is the title and main chorus of the song being analyzed (t/n).

2

Genre Violence[1]: Argentinean Heavy Metal in the Music Market

Luciano Scarrone

Todo es en vano si no hay amor,
desde el artista hasta su contratador.[2]

('Todo es en vano si no hay amor', *Ultimando*, Almafuerte 2003)

Man's New Trajectory

A deep socioeconomic crisis marked the end of the 1980s in Argentina. A new government emerged and, with it, the renewed hope of people who needed to believe in something. In subsequent years, Argentina and the world at large would witness enormous changes as far as the role of the States and the global economy are concerned. These transformations would reverberate in all sectors and activities, including those related to the arts and culture. There were no doubts that in Argentina artists would continue writing, painting, composing and playing music, filming movies, designing choreographies, and dancing. What would radically change, however, was the way in which the production and circulation of those artistic and cultural goods would be structured and managed (Yúdice 2001).

Thanks to bands like Riff and V8, heavy metal became a presence in our country during the 1980s. This presence, however, would be met with the severe disapproval of the media and a society (or at least a substantial part of it) which, at the time, was not prepared to assimilate a new nascent movement intent on reflecting the violent reality of the world. The subsequent decade would find Argentinean heavy metal cementing its reach as an aesthetically and commercially viable musical genre and cultural phenomenon, a sentiment captured in the following lyrics: 'I went about building my identity/dressed in black I forged my ideals/throughout my veins I feel/a true rebellious nature flow' ('Igual Que a Vos', *A.D.N.*, Helker 2010).

Starting from the implicit notion that heavy metal could be catalogued as 'popular music', and understanding the latter category as a wide range of music (initially) defined as *not belonging* to the 'folkloric' or 'classical' music adopted by traditional musicology, studies arose during the final decades of the twentieth century which addressed the diverse concerns surrounding these cultural expressions. Amongst these concerns we can point to the area's interest in the conceptualization of 'genre'. Subsequently, through the disruptive influences of the music market, metal has been segmented and labeled into genres and sub-genres as a sales strategy. As a result, concepts like 'genre' and 'style' merge in a melting pot of groups and artists. Similarly, the semantic frontiers of 'scene' and 'market' also become fused.

From its inception, Argentinean heavy metal – as a musical genre, as a musical scene, as a style, and as a market – has been developing as a field[3] that must be analyzed jointly and contextually. With this objective in mind, I will analyze both the characteristics of the heavy metal market in Argentina as well as the role of its participants over the last twenty years. Additionally, I will consider how the aforementioned concepts interrelate to form and alter the said market.

A Screen into the New World

The period spanning from the 1980s into the early 1990s would see the rise of the digital era around the world. Manuel Castells (1995) has researched and commented about the advancements introduced by the development of information technologies and, with a nod of complicity, introduced the notion of 'the promise' of information and communication technologies, or ICTs.[4] First came the emergence of the compact disc in 1982. Then, in the mid-1990s, the Internet debuted and became a popular platform throughout the world. The music industry saw in the Internet an opportunity to advertise their releases: record companies developed websites dedicated to their artists as a method of promotion. Later on, music began to find an audience on the Internet and this development gave rise to the appearance of online record stores, a development that signaled a revolution for consumers and the record industry. Toward the end of that decade, the appearance of the mp3 format and the first file sharing platforms, which included Napster, would mark a new, highly controversial step in the digitalization era as far as the music industry was concerned. Created in 1999 by Shawn Fanning and Sean Parker as a music files distribution service, Napster became the first large-scale P2P[5] exchange network, its technology allowing users to easily share their mp3 collections with fellow users. During the year 2000, a multitude of recordings, both official and 'pirated', circulated through cyberspace with no control whatsoever on the part of their authors, the performers, or even the record companies and/or publishing houses. One such recording belonged to the band Metallica (arguably the most important group in heavy metal music), who learned that the demo for 'I Disappear', a song that had not been released at the time and which formed part of the *Mission: Impossible 2* movie soundtrack, had somehow found its way into this network, even prompting some radio stations to broadcast this unauthorized version. That same year, Fanning became a defendant in a lawsuit filed in the name of Lars Ulrich, James Hetfield, Kirk Hammett, and Jason Newsted, where the latter requested the removal of their songs from Napster's free service platform. The lawsuit alleged that Napster broke three distinct areas of the law: these were copyright infringement, illegal use of a digital audio platform, and the Racketeering Influence & Corrupt Organizations (RICO) Act. '[T]hey never asked us or other artists if we wanted to participate in their business. It's good that they are going legit' affirmed Lars Ulrich, the band's drummer, after they reached an agreement with the web portal.[6] Over the years, technology has advanced beyond that initial platform, and new ways of 'sharing' music continue to be developed every day. The topic of the legality or lack thereof of this sharing is a matter beyond the purview of this chapter. Still, it is relevant that we analyze these mutations, not as a mere change of the formats in which musical content is commercialized and exchanged, but rather as a cause and consequence of greater transformations that involve various others factors and features. Furthermore, given that we are dealing with transformations that develop around the world, the assimilation and response to these transformations on the part of each location is distinct; thus, considering that this chapter starts with the premise that Argentinean heavy metal is a movement that develops at the margins of the establishment, the possibilities offered by the Internet carry an immense value when it comes to the promotion of this fringe movement.

However, it is paradoxical that, in an age when we are most technologically capable of accessing an immense amount of information, no practical changes have occurred in mainstream public opinion, which continues to be formed and directed at the behest of massive communications corporations. With this in mind, Manuel Castells notes:

> Both historical optimism as well as moral pessimism express, in different tonalities, an equally simplistic message of technological determinism, be it in the liberation of the individual from the restrictions of the local sphere, or in the alienation of a social life that disintegrates into the anonymity of uncontrolled suburban growth.
>
> (Castells 1995: 1)

Regardless, there are alternatives that can challenge this type of binary thinking: one such tool, capable of disrupting the status quo, is this great digital society we have inherited, a society equal parts unstoppable and fiercely dynamic, in which knowledge represents a heritage we must not ignore.

Working toward a more in-depth analysis, it becomes apparent that the transformation of communication systems through the influence of neoliberal processes (privatization, de-regulation, the elimination of services provided by the welfare state for political and economic reasons), enacted during the last decades of the previous century, results in the reformulation and redefinition of territories and audiences. The transnationalization and neoliberalization of the cultural industries impose, first, the need to become part of a supranational economy, and, second, enact various reconfigurations in order to facilitate that very intervention. This responds to 'a dialectic of standardization and differentiation' (Hercovici 1999: 58). On the one hand, legal protocols, technologies, and administrative forms are standardized; on the other hand, adapting to the transnational market requires the creation of local differences that allow for the profitability of content beyond territorial borders.

> Each geographical sector seeks to differentiate itself from its exterior and build its own media image in relation to that exterior in order to prize itself, ultimately looking to enter those same international networks; culture is broadly utilized in the construction of this media image.
>
> (Hercovici 1999: 58–59)

This process, which develops at the heart of industries of culture, is not alien to heavy metal insofar as it is presented as an essential constitutive factor of the phenomenon.[7] In fact, metal music has addressed this concern for the local in its lyrics. Take, for example, the following lyrics from a song by the band A.N.I.M.A.L: 'All that I care for and have cared for is here/friends, feelings rooted in me/nothing could make me forget/that this is my "barrio," this is my "barrio" today' ('Mi Barrio', *Fin de un Mundo Enfermo*, A.N.I.M.A.L. 1994).

This analysis is framed within a widely accepted perception of the heavy metal music originating in our country, which, in fact, enables me to give an account of the existing synergy between the various activities that develop inside and around this field.

Genres, Sub-genres, Styles

> *Punk rock, metal o hardcore, ¿cuándo lo vas a entender?*
> *Es todo música, abrí la cabeza y dejanos de joder.*[8]
>
> ('Tiemposviolentos', *Manteniéndose Real*, Raíz 2001)

Franco Fabbri proposed a description of 'genre' that incorporated factors which, at the time, musicology had not considered. He understood that, although each genre has its own form and style, these were not sufficient to delimit it; therefore, he incorporates in his description of genre the performative techniques, the instrumentation, and the musician's skillset. Each of these can be transmitted through a written code or by way of an oral tradition. Moreover, he identifies a number of social and ideological rules which account for the musician's social image, detail the character of the musical community, and allow for the distinguishing of genres according to the social functions and the different classes, groups, or generations involved. In the same light, he underlines the commercial and juridical rules that comprise the means of production; that is to say, all the aspects comprising the relation between recording and the record companies, copyrights, revenues, promotion, and consumption. In recent years, many theorists have referred to his interpretation and have reflected on and developed the concept of genre (Guerrero 2012).

Simon Frith (2014) has called for an examination of the role of labels in popular music. His argument is that the use of genre categories determines the sales process. The definition of genre is, consequently, linked to the music market: 'Genre is a way of assigning music to its own market, or, alternatively, a market to its own music.... The logic of labelling depends on what the label is for; genre maps change according to who uses them' (2014: 76–77). From here, Frith tries to demonstrate the power radio stations possess in shaping a map of the different genres. Returning to what has already been said about media corporations, we can extend Frith's view and note how, in recent years, 'an image' of Ricardo Iorio[9] has appeared on radio, and especially on television, all while, paradoxically, his work is not (nor has been) disseminated with this same intensity (intentionally, of course). Frith also criticizes Fabbri's approach for being schematic and pretending to achieve a definite delimitation of genres. Genres, Frith argues, are in constant change given the relationships that develop between them.

Keith Negus has addressed the problem of musical genres within the social context and, in particular, the latter's ties to the culture of multinational corporations. His purpose is to analyze 'the way in which categories and musical classification systems condition the music that we could play and listen to, intervening in the musical experience and in its formal organization through the entertainment industry' (2005: 19).

I highlight these theoretical interventions, among many others, mainly because they allow me to discuss how Argentinean heavy metal positions itself in relation to our country's music market. Many authors have reflected – in an academic tone and from a Social Sciences position – on the construction of identities in relation to rock music produced in our country. It is not my intention here to discredit them, nor to blindly join those studies; rather, my intention is to begin a path of open (interdisciplinary) analysis that shows the immense variety of approaches which traverse this cultural phenomenon that, as with the notion of genre, lives within its own heterogeneity and dynamism.

The relationship between the concepts of genre and style is not concretely resolved, nor it is my intention to do so here; instead, my interest is in analyzing the diverse discussions in this area and see how they manifest in the field of Argentinean heavy metal. For the purposes of this chapter, it is convenient that we adopt the definition that sees style as something separate from genre, in so far as it allows us to link a work to an author, a period, a place, or a school; in contrast, genre is limited to a category of classification (Goodman 1990). In heavy metal we can see (listen to), unlike with other musical genres, a *panoply* of styles that, according to the times, have greater or lesser production/repercussion, generally responding to global tendencies.

This is also the case when it comes to the definition of the 'sub-genre' category. López Cano's research focuses on Afro-Cuban music and, even though his genre topic has nothing to do with the one considered here, his analysis fits into this chapter's concerns, particularly when he affirms that 'it is possible to talk about sub-genres in the same way we talk about subsets; thus, if a musical artifact is at the intersection of two or more genres, then this artifact will belong simultaneously to all those genres' (2006: 3). Consequently, one could argue that this definition of sub-genre graphically represents that fusion of genres which, in late 1960s England, gave rise to what today we study, experience, and call heavy metal.

Reinventing Metal

For the development of this analysis, I start with a basic premise, which states that 'industry produces culture and culture produces industry' (Negus 2005: 35). From there I try to analyze the intersection (conceptual and practical) between economy and culture, while also observing the various factors and features that form the field of heavy metal in Argentina. As mentioned above, the temporal focus of this analysis is limited to what has taken place in the last twenty years in our country; therefore, this analysis excludes the years that witnessed the rise of this movement. The reason for this delimitation is directly linked to what occurred in the music industry in Argentina at the start of the 1990s.

It is important to recall that Argentinean heavy metal presents itself as the *appropriation*[10] of a foreign cultural phenomenon and, as such, exhibits characteristics that differentiate it from the same genre and how it developed in other parts of the world.

During the first days of February 1990, two Bon Jovi shows at Vélez Sarsfield Stadium would signal the start of a period of high profile heavy metal concerts (by international artists). This chapter is not interested in taking account of each example or weighing in on the importance of one over the rest; what is worth highlighting here is the notoriety achieved by some national bands that served as supporting bands for these shows, and, perhaps, more importantly, some of the professionalization criteria absorbed by the artists as well as the agents involved in the promotion and commercialization of the heavy metal cultural product.

In speaking about genres, sub-genres, and styles, Argentinian heavy metal music has exhibited a wide gamut of these in its years of existence. Intense arguments and confrontations at the heart of the movement have been overcome over the years and, contrary to what many commentators have tried to cement, these same conflicts have strengthened heavy metal. Within the temporal focus I have delineated, we can mention some of the elements (perhaps the most salient) as a way to offer some examples: Power Metal, Classic Metal, Thrash Metal, Death Metal, Black Metal, Metalcore, Alternative Metal, and Folk Metal have been and remain some of the styles that sustain a scene that, despite its comings and goings, remains decidedly strong. There are those who resist these 'labels', considering them a mere product of the music industry and, as previously noted, they are not entirely wrong in their observation. To analyze the behavior of the individuals involved consider that this industry of culture promotes products through various actions and positions. Even if to a lesser extent when compared to other genres, heavy metal has clearly found a space of belonging within this industry of culture, which, in my estimation, functions as a 'motivating' agent for the enormous amount of underground bands that also comprise and sustain the national scene.

As previously stated, the concept of genre is bound to the market and through radio stations, it directs the promotion of products 'labeled' in advance with that purpose in mind. In Argentina there are some paradigmatic cases when it comes to embodying the role of (specialized) media and its link to metal culture.

Heavy Rock & Pop, a radio program broadcasted through the Rock & Pop station and hosted by Norberto 'El ruso' Verea and Alejandro Nagy between 1991 and 1995, was responsible for bringing to metalheads' ears the music and the news of this ever-growing movement in Argentina. Certainly, there existed (and still exist) alternative or independent stations that granted airtime to heavy metal music in our country, and these have great value in symbolic and representational terms in different regions of the country; but their position when it comes to the market itself is more limited. Following the cessation of *Heavy Rock & Pop*, the same radio station aired *Tiempos Violentos*.[11] This program (which remains on the air to this day) experienced for many years the vast aforementioned changes that took place around the music industry. Without delving too much into the subject, which remains beyond the scope of this study, it could be argued that radio (and all its iterations) lacks the reach it possessed in prior years amongst its listeners, at least when it comes down to its capacity to convey and help build identity, as was the case early on with programs such as *Heavy Rock & Pop*. More recently, in 2012 to be precise, *FM Vorterix* was born. Created by Mario Pergolini, the station would bring about a novel media enterprise which brought together radio, an exhaustive web platform, and a concert hall located in the Colegiales neighbourhood, in the City of Buenos Aires. A physically and symbolically valuable space for heavy metal arose there, not just through the help of the different programs aired on the radio station, but also through the staging of (national and international) concerts at *TeatroVorterix*. Some years prior to this, Carlos Tórtola, a well-known producer and manager in the scene, would create and produce the Metal Para Todos[12] festival; starting in 2012, this festival would be renamed Vorterix Metal Para Todos. The festival has presented seven editions to this day, its settings varying throughout the years; but year after year the festival would present the biggest bands in national heavy metal music, while also setting aside some space for many underground bands. Thus, it can be noted how, to an extent, a small cultural collective has formed around a media outlet composed of several prominent figures of national heavy metal.

Another example worth mentioning here for the way it relates to the goings-on involving specialized media is that of *Madhouse*, a magazine founded in 1989 by writer and journalist César Fuentes Rodríguez, which was distributed throughout all of the country's kiosks, including those in the outskirts, during the peak of the South American scene. The magazine documented the influx of international bands into the Buenos Aires scene, as well as the development of the local milieu and its own movement. It was the first Argentinean magazine within the genre that did not replicate the reports done by the foreign press, instead opting to develop its own articles. A sum of 126 issues were edited before the *corralito*[13] debacle and the economic disaster Argentina endured in December 2001 put an end to this and many other publications. In recent years, *Madhouse*'s place was taken up by *Jedbangers* magazine, a publication under the leadership of Hugo García, who had been a part of Rock & Pop and Vorterix.

As is the case with radio stations, the world of print publications specializing in heavy metal boasts a large number of magazines and fanzines that, despite enjoying less economic power (and therefore a lesser chance for dissemination), have been and continue to be of high symbolic value as it pertains to the formation and consolidation of this peculiar subculture.[14]

The examples highlighted above as well as countless others have been the result of a consumer public demanding a very distinctive product. Time has passed and for different reasons some of these products are no more; but they helped established a way of interacting, and by the mid-1990s, heavy metal culture counted amongst its ranks various important national exponents who had helped set the way forward for the years to come. Heavy metal, which began in the 1980s as an effect (sub-genre) of rock 'pesado',[15] would be established in those early days as a genre that, in turn, would itself spawn various sub-genres and styles already developing for some years in the international scene. Over time (and this holds true to this day), the public and the specialized press would dismantle many of the 'ground rules' regarding the inclusion of new styles and performers involved in the local scene.

It may be the case that, due to its strident sound as well as its musical and (in many cases) lyrical violence, Argentinean heavy metal will always remain at the margins of a music market dominated by the pull of mass consumption. Nevertheless, that 'small' niche, evidence of the space gained in recent years, remains today a strong, active, and dynamic scene, itself a complex cultural movement worthy of being studied from multiple perspectives. 'And without delay or suspicion/consume all that is heavy metal' ('Brigadas Metálicas', *Luchando por el Metal*, V8 1983). This is where we currently stand...

REFERENCES

Almafuerte (2003), *Ultimando*, CD, Argentina: Dejesu.

A.N.I.M.A.L. (1994), *Fin de un Mundo Enfermo*, CD, Argentina: Tommy Gun.

Batalla, Bonfil (1991), 'La teoría del control cultural', *Estudios sobre las Cultural Contemporáneas*, IV:12, pp. 165–204.

Bonfil, Guillermo (1988), 'Teoría del control cultural en los procesos étnicos', *Anuario Antropológico*, Universidade de Brasilia/Tempo Brasileiro, p. 86.

Bordieu, Pierre and Wacquant, Loïc (1995), *Respuestas: Por una Antropología Reflexiva*, Mexico: Grijalbo.

Castells, Manuel (1995), *La Ciudad Informacional: Tecnologías de la Información, Reestructuración Económica y el Proceso Urbano-Regional*, Madrid: Alianza Editorial.

Fabbri, Franco (2006), 'Tipos, categorías, géneros musicales: ¿Hace falta una teoría?', Conference lecture at the VII Congreso IASPM-AL entitled *Música popular: Cuerpo y escena en la América Latina*, celebrated at Havana, 19–24 June, translated by Marta García Quiñones.

Frith, Simon (2014), *Ritos de la Interpretación: Sobre el Valor de la* Música *Popular*, Buenos Aires: Paidós.

Goodman, Nelson (1990), *Maneras de Hacer Mundos*, Madrid: Visor.

Guerrero, Juliana (2012), 'El género musical en la música popular: Algunos problemas para su caracterización', *Trans-Revista Transcultural de Música*, 16., https://www.sibetrans.com/trans/public/docs/trans_16_09.pdf. Accessed 11 February 2020.

Helker (2010), *A.D.N.*, CD, Argentina: Producción Independiente.

Herscovici, Alain (1999), *Globalización, Sistema de Redes y Estructuración del Espacio: Un Análisis Económico*, Buenos Aires: Editorial Biblos.

López Cano, Rubén (2006), 'Asómate por debajo de la pista: Timba cubana, estrategias músico-sociales y construcción de géneros en la música popular', Conference lecture at the VII Congreso IASPM-AL entitled *Música popular: Cuerpo y escena en la América Latina*, celebrated at Havana, 19–24 June.

Negus, Keith (2005), *Los Géneros Musicales y la Cultura de las Multinacionales*, Barcelona: Paidós.

Raíz (2001), *Manteniéndose Real*, CD, Argentina: Estudios Virtuality.

Torreiro, Gustavo (2016), 'El heavy en la Argentina como subcultura: identidad y resistencia' in E. Scaricaciottoli (ed.), *Se Nos Ve de Negro Vestidos*, Buenos Aires, Argentina: Ediciones La Parte Maldita, pp. 21–36.

Yúdice, George (2001), '*La reconfiguración de políticas culturales y mercados culturales en los noventa y siglo XXI en América Latina*', *Revista Iberoamericana*, 67, pp. 639–59.

V8 (1983), *Luchando por el Metal*, LP, Argentina: Umbral.

NOTES

1. The Spanish word 'género' used in the title carries a double meaning. 'Género' in the title refers to the genre of heavy metal; however, the word phrase used in the title originates from issues of gender identity and violence. Given the lack of an English equivalent and the chapter's focus on the topic of genre, this translation will use the genre variant throughout (t/n).
2. 'All is in vain if there is no love/from the artist to their employer' (t/n).
3. According to Bourdieu (1995), a field can be defined as a network or configuration of objective relationships between positions. These positions are objectively defined in their existence and in the determinations they impose upon their occupants, whether they are agents or institutions, by their current and potential situation (situs) in the distribution structure of the different species of power (or capital) – whose possession implies access to the specific winnings that are at stake within the field – and, *en passant*, by the objective relationships with the other positions (domination, subordination, homology, etc.).
4. Although there is no universal definition of ICTs, the term is generally used to mean all devices, networking components, applications, and systems that in combination allow people and organizations to interact in the digital world.
5. *P2P or peer-to-peer*: peer network. A computer network in which all or some aspects work without fixed clients or servers; they act simultaneously as clients and servers in relation to the other network nodes. P2P networks enable direct information exchange, in any format, between connected computers.
6. https://www.rollingstone.com/music/music-news/metallica-napster-settle-236089/. Accessed 11 February 2020.

7. See Torreiro, G. (2016), 'Heavy Metal as a Subculture in Argentina: Identity and Resistance.'
8. 'Punk rock, metal or hardcore, when will you understand?/It's all music, open your mind and stop fucking with us' (t/n).
9. Ricardo Iorio (1962–present) is the most popular artist of the Argentinian heavy metal scene. He founded three important bands in that country: *V8*, *Hermética*, and *Almafuerte*. From 2016 to the present, he has dedicated himself to his solo career.
10. Bonfil Batalla adopts a categorization of 'near' and 'foreign' cultural elements to speak of the 'decisions' enacted upon these. One of the defined categories is 'appropriated culture' which describes the condition 'when the group acquires decision-making capabilities over foreign cultural elements and uses them in acts that respond to their own decisions' (1988: 8).
11. 'Violent Times', which also happens to be the Spanish translation for the title of cult film *Pulp Fiction* by Quentin Tarantino (t/n).
12. 'Metal For All' (t/n).
13. 'Playpen', informal name given to the policy of freezing bank accounts and other economic measures taken by the Argentinean government at the end of 2001, which led to one of the country's worst crisis in its history (t/n).
14. The term subculture is employed in sociology, anthropology, and cultural studies to define a group of people with a distinctive set of behaviors and beliefs that differentiate them from the dominant culture to which they are attached. See Torreiro, Gustavo. 'Heavy Metal in Argentina as a Subculture: Identity and Resistance'.
15. That is, hard rock. The Spanish equivalent was used early on, but has been gradually substituted by the English nomenclature (t/n).

3

Heavenly Hosts and Other Demons: Reflections Concerning a Difficult and Transversal Relationship in the History of Our Heavy Music[1]

Gito Minore

The year 1986 heralds a paradigm shift in the incipient history of Argentinean heavy metal. Overwhelmed by endless obstacles that prevented the soon-to-be 'mother of all bands' from progressing in an increasingly decimated metal scene, plagued by a series of problems aggravated by the consumption of alcohol and drugs, and after serious internal fissures, some members of the band V8 would convert to Christianity, or, to be more precise, Evangelicalism.

From that moment, the band's growing popularity was affected by the reaction of a public who could not comprehend, at first glance, what this about-face was all about. Those individuals who until recently had opened themselves up to scrutiny on and off stage, brandishing lyrics like the ones contained in 'La Mano Maldita'[2] and 'Deseando Destruir y Matar',[3] suddenly found themselves in the midst of a 'reborn' musical collective intent on preaching sermons which included the recital, without warning, of Psalm 58, or the utterance, to a small and confused audience, of lyrics that included the following: 'now I truly understand that/with God present here/my soul will never die'.

It did not take long before condemnation against this abrupt change reverberated throughout the scene. They were accused of being 'sellouts', 'going soft' and a host of other nastier charges. These attacks grew especially loud when they took it upon themselves to wander around some temples, making the rounds as 'repentant flagellants' recounting their *affaires* with past temptations.

This sudden turn, coupled with the fast growth in popularity of white metal groups from the United States (Stryper among them), sowed uncertainty amongst a throng of heavy metal adherents. After all, many had initially adopted the style because of the rebellious nature and indelible confrontational attitude the scene had promised. This being the case, a retrospective look at this complicated period in Argentinian metal history, in which our heavy metal gave its first steps towards what we would call a novel democracy, all within the context of a bifurcated world panorama inserted within the violent margins of the Cold War, affords the chance to, if not shed new light, then at least propose new questions.

Taking into account the history of North America's use of the Evangelical movement as a tool deployed toward the submission of Latin American countries, this work will consider and question how much of an influence State policy and individual personal development respectively played into the incursion and rise of a subgenre in our country. To what extent was V8's conversion a personal spiritual choice and how much of it was steeped in historical indoctrination methods? To what extent was this (perhaps naive) initial acceptance of newfound faith later followed through to its maturation? Did they really follow through on it? Finally, can it be legitimately argued that V8 is the origin of white metal or Christian rock in Argentina?

American Imperialist Evangelicalism and the Birth of White Metal

It could be argued that, from the moment human beings began evolving as such on the face of the earth, their relationship with divinities, initially rooted in their surrounding nature but developing increasingly toward abstraction (culminating in the belief of a single omnipresent and invisible God), was inevitable and even necessary.

Few would deny that, to a certain extent, humanity has come to define itself through this fundamental relationship. The subject is precisely *a* subject because two worlds converge in them: on the one hand, the subject lives in the world of matter, flesh, somatosensory experience, the natural world shared with mammals; and, on the other hand, the subject also lives in the spiritual world, the one which, in their quest for identity, they have built in the march towards evolution.

The relationship of this spiritual world with art equally transverses the history of humanity; after all, art serves to glorify the spiritual world, simultaneously wading in its waters in search for inspiration. A simple look at any moment of Antiquity, the Middle Ages, or Modernity is all it takes to come face to face with artists, both prominent and lesser-known, who have combined both the physical and the spiritual world. Art, in and of itself, serves as the great catalyst of these two apparently opposite universes.

Within Hegelian phenomenology, art is rightfully the first articulation of the consciousness of the Spirit (which has its apex in Greek sculpture); in this same system, art will later be surpassed by religion (the Christian monotheistic tradition being the most pervasive, according to Hegel), and these articulations will eventually reach their apogee with philosophy. This very fact often leads to the conflation of art with spirituality, the former not understood as the search for meaning for its own sake, but rather as the effect of a particular religious practice. In the case of the west, this relationship takes place particularly within the Christian religion, more precisely within Catholicism.

Heavy metal, as an artistic phenomenon, is no stranger to this fact. Specifically, because of its characteristics, it has had, since its inception, a close relationship with Christianity. As sociologist Deena Weinstein asserts in the film *Metal: A Headbanger's Journey*, 'If Christianity did not exist, heavy metal as we know it would not exist. Religion is truly crucial in this'.[4]

The presence of Christianity is noticeable in the iconoclastic imagery deployed in album covers, as well as in the references contained in song lyrics. The imagery, which includes crosses, symbols, and a multitude of outfits from different eras of the Christian tradition, is also present in the creation of the apparel and the look adopted by the musicians and their followers. One highly visible and influential use of the cross in metal, for example, originated with Black Sabbath, pillars of the movement, from whom most of the trends that will eventually develop far and wide across the world derive.

Heavy metal would expand across the globe, with lesser or greater diffusion, in turn creating subgenres in which the Christian influence is present. This is clearly the case in Nordic countries, where black metal, or more specifically Norwegian black metal, was directly defined by this relationship with Christianity, obviously situating itself in clear opposition.

In Argentina, heavy metal, from its very inception, remained closer to its true origins; that is to say, it served as a musical response on the part of the more neglected classes. As was the case with heavy metal in Birmingham during the early 1970s, heavy metal in Argentina found a niche in its increasingly deteriorated industrial belt; in their case, this means Greater Buenos Aires, particularly toward the west and in the south. From there it did not take long for metal to spread to the rest of the provinces, each one imbuing it with its own specific problems. In the case of Argentinean heavy metal, we have also come to define our relationship with Christianity. Here the relationship was one of criticism, mainly of the clergy and the leadership of the institution, and its links to economic and political power, which at that moment had begun to disassociate itself from military power (that is, if it ever truly did).

Nevertheless, the most prominent or at least most publicized type of heavy metal music was neither ours nor the Nordic one; it was not even the English one. It was the one originating from the United States. The kind of heavy metal created there, which was widely disseminated across the world, was more aligned with pop culture and capitalist consumption than with its more intellectual or oppositional relationship with religion.

North American metal, at least the most popular and best-selling type,[5] was characterized by its more inconsequential lyrics, which put greater emphasis on excesses, obscenity, and over-the-top sensuality, themes that were not incompatible with heavy metal in general, but which in this particular iteration and its constant abuse of these themes turned the genre into something pornographic.

It must be noted that heavy metal was not the only locus of this type of incitement, though it was probably its most visible scapegoat. Pop stars such as Prince and Madonna became purveyors of equal excess. All these examples that were being disseminated throughout the world, of role models for adolescents and juveniles, nonetheless, became a cause for concern for the conservative housewives of North American society.

Thus, in the year 1985, two women married to prominent figures in positions of power – Tipper Gore (wife of democrat Al Gore, later vice-president during the Clinton years) and Susan Baker (wife of Treasury Secretary James Baker) founded the PMRC (Parents Music Resource Center). Its stated mission was to 'alert parents about their children's musical consumption'. However, its ulterior objective was to control the youth, tame it in accordance to Christian ideals, and prevent any deviations from the norm whatsoever. Pop music and its derivatives were, perhaps, seen as the lesser threat; heavy metal, on the other hand, with its provocative message, would conceivably lead many to fear the possibility of some kind of rebellious insurrection, one that needed to be quelled before it had a chance to even begin.

The public hearings against various musicians of the time, which in hindsight were nothing but a bona fide witch-hunt, attained a level of notoriety; in them, figures like the brilliant Dee Snider of Twisted Sister excelled, with the trials ultimately resulting in the implementation of the now-famous Parental Advisory sticker.

It is worth recalling that, during that same period, a band burst into the metal scene which successfully capitalized, through its foundational concept, on the desires of these 'noble' people. That band's name is Stryper. Formed in 1983 in Orange County, CA, the band managed to fuse the prevailing glam aesthetics – i.e., teased hair, tight clothing, and catchy metal music – with lyrics heavily emphasizing Christian beliefs. Their first album, *Soldiers under Command*, recorded in 1985, was merely a harbinger of the success they would achieve a year later with their best-selling album, *To Hell with the Devil*. The record reached platinum status, selling over one million copies.

A throng of young people, led by these alluring pied pipers, filled stadiums singing hymns that invited them to choose a clearly defined road: 'Choose your own destiny/free to open up/and believe' ('Free'). A different song offered the following invitation: 'Oh, What did you say?/Oh, Christ is the way' ('The Way'). And if these were not sufficiently direct, within that same album, they made it clear for their audience which land was the promised land that God had specifically chosen for this freedom to occur: 'In a land of freedom/God has sent his grace/We're proud to live in such a place' ('Sing Along Song').

The aforementioned record, which through the graphic violence depicted in its cover invited audiences to renounce the devil, the latter responsible for all evil, would be followed by an homonymous documentary film. The film starts with a voice-over of one of their fans reading a letter she wrote to the band:

> Dear Stryper: My name is Melissa and I'm 15 years old. I'm writing to you to thank you for saving me from the Devil. For many years, I was unhappy and even thinking about suicide until I heard your music. I knew then that God was speaking to me through your music. I was so lost but now I'm on the road to a real Christian life of God's love and happiness. [...] I owe my life to you.
>
> (Postma, 1989)

The moving testimony of the alleged Melissa is not the only one but, rather, one of the many that are interspersed throughout and which share the same tenor; in addition, the documentary includes some anecdotes by the musicians and footage of live performances. In one of these clips, we witness the singer shouting with his high-pitched voice 'Stryper sings in the name of Jesus Christ' while the guitarist throws bibles from stage to their feverish audience. Meanwhile, on stage, a cross made of lights shines on them, while the group's name is showcased in big letters, accompanied by the epigraph 'Isaiah 53:5'. If we look at the New King James version of *The Bible*, we find that the epigraph reads: 'But he was wounded for our transgressions, He was bruised for our iniquities; The chastisement for our peace was upon him, and by His stripes we are healed'.

A more recent version of the bible, *The Christian Standard Bible*, which depended on the input of hundreds of scholars for a more accurate translation of the original text, uses 'rebellions' when discussing the 'transgressions' spoken about in the NKJ version. This allusion to a rebellion is equally present in the

Reina de Valera Spanish version. Although few would deny that it is somewhat unsettling, perhaps it would be hasty at this point to focus on the word 'rebellions' and what role this notion plays as a footnote to the name of a band that sold, at the time, the impressive sum of one million albums. That is why, for the time being, it is preferable to take one slight detour before returning to the matter at hand.

From the Stripes to the Open Veins

Once the herd was under control at home, the next step was to take care of the stragglers, i.e., Latin America as a whole. There, reality was a little more complicated; it was not a matter of bringing down some *glam* guy's coif, washing the face of some sorcerer's pseudo-apprentice, or concealing an opulent model's nipples. Not at all.

The onset of World War II produced a provisional distancing between the so-called developed or industrialized nations and those at the periphery. This new reality brought about, as it is generally accepted, the rise of nationalist and revolutionary movements. In response to this, Alfredo Silleta notes, 'Imperialism, fully recovered by the mid-fifties, will subdue most of these movements and reassert its hold over the region' (1986: 141). In response to this new order of things, a segment of the ecclesiastical Curia would move to adopt a historically unprecedented and defining change. For the first time in Latin American history, the Catholic Church proposed a different interpretation of the gospel, a move which brought them closer to the poor, to the detriment of the oligarchies and the powerful with whom they had collaborated from the moment they initially arrived at our shores. This new proposal created what is now known as the 'liberation theology' and became a religious endorsement of many of our revolutions. Obviously, this new stance by the Catholic Church greatly displeased the Northern powers. So much so that, in light of all this, during the year 1969 an outline was developed for what would eventually be known as 'The Rockefeller Report'.[6] This thick document laid out the Latin American situation of the time. According to Silleta (1986: 143–44), in his chapter 'The Cross and The Sword' of the text mentioned above, the document states that

> [c]urrently, the Church may be, in many ways, in the same situation as the youths: exhibiting a profound idealism but, as a result, in some cases, vulnerable to subversive influences, ready to support a revolution if necessary in order to end injustice.

Determining that the Church was no longer a trustworthy ally for the United States, the report, according to Silleta, went on to recommend that the US government 'provide support to fundamentalist Christian groups or churches like those led by Sun Myung Moon (Unificationism) and the Hare Krishnas, as a means to counter the nascent liberation theology'.

As a result, during the late 1960s and early 1970s, Latin America was literally invaded by these types of sects and churches rooted in Pentecostalism which advocated for a return to individualism, condemned collectivism, saw communism and Satanism as one and the same, and, in the face of such a chaotic world, proposed that its followers disregard said world, given that, in their view, there was no point in fighting for a civilization that precedes the apocalypse. It is worth noting the way authors such as Jean-Pierre Bastian downplay the idea that the emergence of these groups was due to the fact that they were financed by North American capital interests, instead believing their rise was the result of the Catholic Church's own failings. Contemptuously calling them a 'religious racket', Bastian affirms that 'the novelty of the pentecostal and millenarian phenomenon does not reside in exogenous contributions, nor in its endogenous characteristics, but rather in its development on the margins of institutional Catholicism and, likewise, of historical Protestantism' (2007: 187).

Nevertheless, and aside from the belittling contempt, there are multiple thinkers and data that support the theory expressed above by Silleta. As he himself affirms: 'In February 1985, the Brazilian Episcopal Conference called attention to what they saw as the political meaning of the expansion of the new sects and their ultimate purpose'. According to the bishops, 'the CIA would be supporting fundamentalist and violently anticommunist groups, both evangelical as well as oriental (sic), to hinder the progressive Church's actions' (1986: 146). A similar argument has been espoused, from a different side of the Christian divide, by the Reverend Raúl Suárez (2011), director of Editorial Caminos in La Habana, in the prologue the important study entitled *Exporting North American Gospel* (Brouwer et al. 2011). In this study, Súarez reasserts Domingo Riorda's arguments in his article 'A Summary with Questions' published in the Ecumenical press on November 2011. Suárez posits:

> With regards to evangelicals, questions emerge about that which has remained unspoken; mainly, their intimate ties with ideological attitudes linked to the political right wing of powerful sectors in the United States. They were actively 'anti' Nicaragua, and 'anti' El Salvador in the 1970s, which included the provision of weapons for the 'Contras'; they supported Pinochet and had a major influence in Fujimori's election; and they similarly applied and continue to apply that same ideological vision to their political participation throughout different

> countries in the continent. The case of Guatemala is illustrative. There, they promoted and became infatuated with the arrival, by way of a coup d'état, of José Efraín Ríos Montt, minister of the 'Church of the Word' who, in 1982, would become the worst Guatemalan dictator.
>
> (7–8) [For more information on this subject please see: *Conferencia Episcopal Argentina* (1979), and Dri (2000, 2004).]

These assertions, added to those stated earlier, encapsulate the leading role those in power in the United States took to suffocate any collective uprising that sought to rebel, control, and subjugate those countries ruled by sinister dictatorships and, in the event anything remained in the aftermath, to impose a culture, a true philosophy of submission to their precepts. For these purposes they benefited from the support of evangelical churches and new technologies, including television and radio, which operated in their favor.

Consequently, along with the financing of these 'evangelizing missions', we see the arrival and spread of the so-called *televangelists*, agents whose job it is to disseminate these indoctrinating messages into the chaste solitude of each family's home. Thus, the so-called 'Transnational Religious Movements' had as their primary objective the dismantling of the most important revolutions; this included the Sandinista revolution in Nicaragua. In the case of the Sandinistas, they sought to undermine the role of its theoretical basis, the 'liberation theology', as popularized in the Puebla Conference Document of 1979.

A new challenge would subsequently appear for right wing theoreticians in the United States. May 1980, according to Silleta, saw 'the drafting of the Santa Fe Document, a document that will become the basis of the religio-political doctrine of Reagan's conservative platform' (1986: 148). Once in power, the new right, brought together in 1977 thanks to the 'Transnational Religious Movements', expands on the work initiated some years earlier. Thus, 'in less than ten years, they successfully managed to control five radio and television networks with over 40 television channels and 1500 radio stations, reaching an audience of forty million North Americans' (1986: 155).

This remotely controlled, bona fide electronic brainwasher exponentially multiplied faith-based audiences, with throngs of faithful continuing to slowly add up. In our country, it had its first presence with *The 700 Club*, which was broadcasted by Channel 9. From that point forward the incursion did not stop and, today, these groups possess several channels and radio stations not only in the City of Buenos Aires but in the provinces as well, boasting millions in operational capital.

With all this in mind, it is not hard to imagine and surmise what role the conversion of heavy metal youth to this type of Christianity could potentially play for these groups. To push Stryper toward stardom and promote them in North American, as well as Latin American societies – while alleging that the move was intended solely to win back the souls of the youth and nothing else – served not just as a chance to promote fake morality, but it was also a way to undermine any possible rebellion.

V8 at a Crossroad

Argentina was no stranger to the role of evangelicals in political coups. From 1976 to 1982, the country endured one of the most ferocious dictatorships anywhere, which resulted in the sum of 30,000 disappeared individuals and thousands of exiled Argentinians. After such a dark moment, the restoration of democracy in 1983 was marked by the painful 'uncovering' of the dictatorship's crimes and (some allege) a newfound 'libertinism' out of which grew a plethora of new musical groups with varied offerings.

Many of these bands were guided by an attraction to senseless amusement, escapism, and hedonism. With the influx of a variety of drugs during those years, the cultural landscape of Buenos Aires saw the proliferation of a vernacular centered on drug use; this included the circulation of song lyrics which specifically spoke about them. Los Redondos, Soda Stereo, Charly García, and many other bands and soloists, several of whom would subsequently enjoy prominent careers, participated in this new vernacular.[7]

It is within this climate that Argentinean heavy metal takes its first steps. In this nascent manifestation of heavy metal, a band stands out on the strength of its own merits, becoming a towering force in later years: that band is none other than V8. Formed in the late 1970s after a noisy presentation in one of the most important shows of the time (B.A. Rock), the band records its first LP in the year 1983, entitled *Luchando por el Metal*,[8] followed shortly afterwards by their sophomore effort, *Un Paso más en la Batalla*.[9] Not only did they set themselves apart from their peers in terms of their sound – one that was much more brutal and raw – but also in the lyrical content of their songs. While the rest of the music 'industry' had its mind on more frivolous matters, as we noted earlier, V8 aimed to criticize and admonish the system by reflecting back the latter's own weaknesses and deficiencies. It must be noted that they were not the only group within the genre to focus on these concerns, but, arguably, it was the most acclaimed. Thus, in spite of all the obstacles, the group cemented its own place in the history of Argentinean music.

Nevertheless, at the beginning of 1986 the band began to go through one if its most trying times. After some years ardently working the scene, and following a failed attempt to establish themselves in the Brazilian scene, Ricardo Iorio and

Alberto Zamarbide, the group's co-founders, decided to dismiss two of the original members: Osvaldo Civile and Gustavo Rowek. The decision grew out of the former's frustration with the sloppiness, lack of effort, and abuse of alcohol and drugs of the latter. In that decision to replace members, one could see the tip of even greater problems affecting the group; existential, emotional, and economical problems were taking their toll. During the remodeling, Miguel Roldán joined the band; upon joining the band, Roldán, along with Zamarbide, converts to evangelicalism. In addition to these conversions, Iorio's growing interest in the teachings of the Basilio Scientific School led the band down new roads. In this climate, the band started writing the songs that will become part of a crucial record in the history of Argentinean heavy metal: *El Fin de los Inicuos*.[10]

Because of its lyrical content (religion as a theme is exceedingly highlighted) and the accompanying preaching on the part of those members who converted to evangelicalism, the record is often remembered as V8's 'evangelical record' or their 'Christian album'. A quick listen of this record is enough to lead anyone to surmise that this could very well be an antecedent to white metal in Argentina, or, at the very least, an attempt at introducing this subgenre in our country. If we recall the North American heavy metal origin story established above – a story linked to sex, drugs, and a penchant for notoriety – and if we consider the fact that from its inception heavy metal in Argentina was seen as something linked to violence, it would not be farfetched to imagine the possibility that this album was an attempted takeover of the genre. However, in truth, this record, for various reasons, responds to a different set of needs. Let us approach this on a step-by-step basis.

Before we start analyzing the album's lyrics, it is imperative that we emphasize not only our need to remember Zamarbide and Roldán's conversion to the evangelical faith, but that we constantly keep in mind Iorio's already mentioned interest in the Basilio Scientific School. The tension or tensions that form the thematic center of the album will reside at the intersection of both fronts.

If we follow Ana Mourín's assessment – she notes that 'save for the song "Trágico Siglo", whose author is A. Zamarbide, and the Psalm 58, taken from the Bible and adapted to music composed by M. Roldán, the remaining songs that make up the record are authored by R. Iorio' (1993: 51) – we can reach some conclusions with regards to *El Fin de los Inicuos*. Through its guiding principles, the Basilio Scientific School seeks a return to an appreciation of God through the teachings of Jesus of Nazareth. One of the reasons the original message has been distorted, according to this belief, has to do with the Roman Catholic Church's success in becoming the hegemonic institution defining Jesus' message. To reach their objectives, the founders of this current propose a method that attains knowledge through the use of our own human faculties; these include spiritualism.[11]

Through this rubric we can read the lyrics of this album, which, as Mourín notes, 'were subjected to modifications made by Zamarbide and Roldán, who expressed dissatisfaction with specific words or phrases used by Iorio' (1993: 51). Nevertheless, aside from the documented evidence of change noted in 'No enloqueceré' (later re-recorded by Almafuerte in the album *Mundo Guanaco* as 'Voy a enloquecer'[12]) we have no other document to analyze other than the album itself. However, on its own the album, we will argue, provides substantial evidence for this analysis.

Upon first reading these lyrics, we encounter a strong indictment of the Catholic Church. One example of this is the song 'La Gran Ramera',[13] which makes clear reference to verse 17 of the Apocalypse; the song blames the institution for its role in man's perdition. The accusation becomes apparent during the last segment: 'Man will again love/when you are no more/His mind will be free/the exterior will die out/with the injustice/that came out of your womb'. Through a similar apocalyptic rubric, we can interpret the song 'Ciega Ambición'[14]: 'The divine prophesy/is being fulfilled/and discontent/increases the disorder'.

Notoriously, the target of these as well as the majority of the record's lyrics is the Catholic Church. Unlike other nations in Latin America, where church leadership operated as a subversive agent against those in power, in Argentina the church was and still remains an ally to those in power, power which at the time and until recently rested in the hands of the military. The band's criticism is also present in 'El Vivo Sustento del Inquisidor',[15] where the philosophy of the Scientific School shines through: 'Connect your existence to the Creator/who gave us our existence/so as to isolate you from evil and its errors/and allow you to live again'.

The invitation to reassess a life lived through the influence of divinity over other false conceptions is also present in the song 'Antes que los Viejos Reyes'.[16] The song lyrics state: 'Destroy your hours thinking, before the old kings/intone a false anthem of love/and its radiance burns innocent souls'.

Another core idea on the record is the condemnation of egoism. This is best appreciated in the album's title track: 'In due time the end of the iniquitous will come/for their ignorance keeps them in their own egoism/only the light of the creator will judge them'. This song establishes a seamless conversation with the topic of greed tackled in 'Reina Ciega'.[17] In it, the lyrics state 'I woke up seeing the blind queen/wallowing in the mud/[...]/she relishes in her evil ways/for she knows not how to love'.

Also noteworthy here is the band's inclusion of a biblical text; in their hands, Psalm 58 becomes a prayer demanding the punishment of the wicked: 'The righteous will rejoice when he is avenged/his feet will bathe in the blood of the wicked'. Furthermore, if we follow the Psalm's line of reasoning, it would seem that 'the wicked' here are indeed the church's institutional members: 'From the womb the wicked went astray/spreading lies from within'.

The song 'Trágico Siglo',[18] the only one written by Zamarbide, demands a different analysis. In it, the thread that united Iorio's lyrics (i.e., indictment of the ecclesiastic institution, condemnation of egoism, search of spirituality without mediators) is absent. In its place there is a return to the eschatology on the cross, strongly rejected by the Scientific School ('A great sacrifice/on the cross he made for me/the blood of the Christ/covered by my affliction'); additionally, we simultaneously find a tendency highly valued by evangelicalism, the *Deux ex machina* effect, which will be a core precept guiding the analysis of Logos' first CD, *La Industria del Poder*,[19] a notion we will return to shortly. The following serves as a clear sample of these dominants in the song: 'Raising signs/they announce their coming/the heavenly hosts/of the end of times'. Comparing these diametrically opposed lyrical styles, we can see that, although the search for a spiritual answer was budding, in no way did this search have a single, monolithic answer, as an evangelical reading would imply. Far from being a presentation defined from a particular faith, the album is rather a question, or a series of questions.

In the face of an Argentina decimated by the recently suffered dictatorship and lost in an alleged democracy, V8's answer was not the placid complacency of the escapism promoted by rock in general, but, rather, a spiritual search; a question about who we are. However, in that moment it was very difficult to analyze it from that point of view. The album's poor sales, coupled with the sermonizing Zamarbide threw himself into in the midst of their shows – as documented both by Mourín in the book and by Joaquín Amat on his YouTube archive of performance videos from the era[20] – resulted in turning it into a ridiculed piece rather than a serious object of study. *El Fin de los Inicuos* was V8's last record. After a couple of presentations hampered by much discord, the band dissolved.

Logos: Between Faith and Permanent Vindications

Split by irreconcilable stances, the two leaders and founders of the original V8 went their separate ways. Iorio, for his part, established Hermética, a band whose name in itself signals a philosophical inclination linked to some religious cults. Even though, as any listener can ascertain, faith as a theme is not the main lyrical concern in the band's corpus, it is nonetheless still present, especially when it comes to their critical interventions. This critical approach is of particular notoriety in the song 'Desde el Oeste'[21] off of their first record: 'Everything is darkness/someone approaches me/I can't tell if it's an evangelist or a policeman'.

The table had already been set when it came to their treatment of the Catholic Church, which continued to be their primary target; however, now they added to their attacks the burgeoning Pentecostal groups, which were gaining a more prominent role in Argentina.

As we previously explained, these churches started making inroads in Latin America during the 1980s thanks in large part to the support of the Reagan administration, who saw them as a way to maintain control of the region. In Argentina, this trend began its spread at the end of the decade but became popularly cemented in the 1990s. During that period, the evangelical message benefited from access to television spaces where someone like Pastor Giménez (among others) excelled; additionally, many former cinema houses were converted into new temples. Meetings were held in these buildings at various times of the day. Even more outstanding was the practice of youth assemblies, which took place at midnight on Saturdays in places like the Flores neighborhood in Buenos Aires. These assemblies were far from being a random occurrence, particularly when we consider the fact that, before the meetings, many young evangelicals informally organized would go out into nearby streets to hand out flyers, inviting everyone to come and 'listen to good music and have a free coffee'. As a matter of fact, many devotees would find their way into the Church this way, for they were generally young people in a state of vulnerability.

In some of these temples, one could even find members of the now-defunct V8 mingling with the crowd, narrating their experiences to anyone who would listen. It is because of practices like this one that one can see the validity of the comparison made by Iorio in the song mentioned above. To claim that Zamarbide and the rest of the band were victims of a Machiavellian ploy to ensnare more adepts into the cult is surely an exaggeration, for at the time they were simply not as famous as they would later become; but there can be no doubt that they were exploited nonetheless, like any other simpleton.

After some time on this path, and after capitalizing on some of these experiences, the band Logos is born and their debut album *La Industria del Poder* hits the streets. A quick analysis of the album's lyrical content can give us a sense of just how committed the group's members were to their faith at the time.

The first track of the album, authored by the three former members of V8, illustrates the ideas I have been developing throughout this chapter. 'Marginado'[22] is the story of a prototypical young man of the 1990s – alone, lost, and persecuted by the ill-tempered police of the time. It is this subject –the aimless, despised, and socially condemned youth – who is addressed not only by the song, but by the album in its entirety. The final part of the song's lyrics serves as a counter-proposal of sorts on the part of the group, a slogan which could have served as an effective advertisement for the temples: 'When you feel tired/and nobody hears your voice/God will be by your side/to feel your pain'. Through the prism of this lyric, we can read the rest of the material. One of the most particular elements that characterizes the group's output, present at the end of this song but mainly at the end of other lyrics and that we outlined in the previous section, is their use of the *deux ex machina motif*. Literally, the term means 'god from the machine'. The term has its origin in Greek and Roman theater, where a contraption allowed a deity to enter from outside the stage in order to solve a situation. Nowadays, the term refers to those situations, many times lacking in logic and coherence with regards to the story, in which a 'savior' is employed to give the tale a conclusion. In our case, we will return to the figure that gives the term its name, i.e., God himself; after all, it is through the figure of God and his interventions that most of the record can be read.[23] In reaction to a Humanity that moves aimlessly forward, victims of their own vanity, the Lord will spectacularly appear: 'Like lightning in the dark/Like lightning in the night he will come/seeking out those to whom he swore eternity'. Likewise, in the catchy 'Ven a la Eternidad',[24] it is Christ himself who not only solves the injustices but who also beckons the listener: 'Come towards eternity/if you can believe/that I am life itself/You shall never die/for on the cross/I defeated death'.

It is worth noting that the subject of these songs is cast into a passive role. He suffers from injustices against which he can do nothing; all he can do is wait for Providence to take care of his situation. And in the case of *El fin de los inicuos,* this is something that never happens. However, the youth is granted a glimmer of hope in the shape of a potential resistance. A clear example of this occurs in the songs 'No te Rindas'[25] and at the end of the album, in the homonymously titled 'Resiste a Morir'.[26] Even though salvation ultimately comes from the hand of God, resisting, enduring, and not giving up will be man's attributes, an aspect which follows to some extent the heavy metal logic of the first V8 records.

Another salient aspect of the record is the apocalyptic tone that permeates the songs. Hatred, misery, division, and egoism are present throughout the record, but are particularly highlighted in songs like 'La Última Batalla'[27] and 'En la Ciudad Violenta'.[28]

The record is a clear snapshot of the period capturing what the members of *Logos* were living through and feeling back then. However, it should be noted that this album did not have any successors of the same tenor. Even when their presentations and concerts were within the same scene as the heavy metal bands of the moment (Cemento, Die Schule, Viejo Correo), they were far from being an evangelical band to the letter.

The lyrics of *Generación Mutante*,[29] the follow-up to *El Fin de los Inicuos*, follows a philosophical line that aligns more to the first V8 record than to the evangelical worldview. Instead of focusing on God and his promise of a marvelous salvation, this record is more concerned with describing and analyzing other issues. Technological apocalypse, the triumph of the machine, dehumanization, criticism of the System, rejection of the police, and social vindications, including those of a Latin American bent, prevail in an album that greatly distances itself from the first one.

And Now, What?

As stated at the beginning of this chapter, heavy metal and religion have a close relationship. This includes 'aesthetics', so to speak, but also links on a deeper level to a common place of searching, of understanding and defining human beings. Exhibiting both positive and negative qualities, V8's *El Fin de los Inicuos* and Logos' *La Industria del Poder* saw the bands venture into a dangerous territory littered with traps. Taking into account the imperialist machinations described on the first part of this chapter and their links with mass media, along with the invention of white metal, we can better understand the magnitude and seriousness of the problem at hand.

However, in spite of these links, we can conclude that Argentinean heavy metal enjoys a particularly privileged position. The fact that metal in Argentina has never been a genre with mass appeal, as has been the case in other countries (most notably in the United States during the 1980s), makes it, in a way, an uninviting tool for 'transnational', large scale operations.

There are countless reasons we could offer that would justify linking each band's lyrical output to any (Christian) religious institution; this becomes particularly the case once we analyze the tensions between the lyrics composed by Iorio and Zamarbide in *El Fin de los Inicuos*. At the same time, in spite of the strong religious bent prevailing in the album *La Industria del Poder*, linking the album with 'militant evangelicalism' would be to engage in overreach. One could argue that this was an endeavor the ex-V8 members either did not know how to carry out or were not interested in carrying out.

I lean toward the latter option. Although it is bathed in Christian idealism, the record, being the only one in their career with such an outspoken evangelical position, is more of a snapshot than a manifesto, an agenda that, due to heavy metal's own limitations and the personal intentions and quests of a group of independent musicians, was impossible to carry out under those conditions and at that time.

The unfortunate task of spreading Christianity to the masses was ultimately taken up, not by Argentinean heavy metal, but, rather, by rock music. This is demonstrated by bands such as R.E.S.C.A.T.E. (gospel band that in the late 1990s performs a crossover into popular rock which catapults them to the top of national and Latin American charts) and Kyosco. An analysis of their output would shed further light on the 'Christian Rock' phenomenon. But doing so would exceed the limits of the present chapter.

REFERENCES

Barker, Emma (1991), *Dancing with the Devil*, TVF.

Bastian, Jean-Pierre (2007), 'El papel político de los protestantes en América', in G. Kepel (ed), *Las Políticas de Dios*, Bogotá: Editorial Norma, pp. 179–96.

Brouwer, Steve, Gifford, Paul and Rose, Susan (2001), *Exportando el Evangelio Norteamericano: El Fundamentalismo Cristiano Global*, La Habana: Editorial Caminos.

Conferencia Episcopal Argentina (ed.) (1979), *La Evangelización en el Presente y en el Futuro de América Latina. Documento de Puebla*, Buenos Aires: Argentina.

Dri, Rubén (2000), *La Utopía de Jesús,* Buenos Aires: Editorial Biblos.

Dri, Rubén (2004), *El movimiento Antiimperial de Jesús*, Buenos Aires: Editorial Biblos.

Dunn, Sam (2005), *Metal: A Headbanger's Journey*, Tornoto: Banger Films.

Hermética (1989), *Hermética*, CD, Argentina: Radio Trípoli.

——— (1991), *Ácido Argentino*, CD, Argentina: Radio Trípoli.

Logos (1993), *La Industria del Poder*, CD, Argentina: DBN.

——— (1996), *Generación Mutante*, CD, Argentina: DBN.

——— (1998), *Tercer Acto*, CD, Argentina: NEMS Enterprises.

Mourin, Ana (1993), V8: Un Sentimiento, Buenos Aires: Independiente.

Postma, Laurens (1989), *To Hell with the Devil*, London: Yo-yo Films.

Silleta, Alfredo (1986), *Las Sectas Invaden la Argentina*, Buenos Aires: Editorial Contrapunto.

Suárez, Raúl (2011), 'Prólogo', in S. Brouwer, P, Gifford, and S. Rose (eds), *Exportando el Evangelio Norteamericano. El Fundamentalismo Cristiano Global*, La Habana: Editorial Caminos, pp. 5–10.

V8 (1986), *El Fin de los Inicuos*, CD, Argentina: DBN.

NOTES

1. Hosts: huestes. Unless otherwise noted, the use of hosts in this article refers to 'army, troops, hordes'.
2. 'The Cursed Hand' (t/n).
3. 'Yearning to Destroy and Kill' (t/n).
4. *Metal. A Headbanger's Journey*, film by Sam Dunn, 2005.
5. It is worth mentioning that, although they were still not very acclaimed or influential, during that the same period and in that same country, Megadeth, Slayer, and the first wave of thrash metal bands were beginning to develop, a subgenre that would fully distance itself from the themes covered by the other subgenres already mentioned.
6. The Rockefeller report on the Americas, Quadrangle Books, New York Times edition, 1969 (t/n).
7. One exception we should mention is the band Los Violadores, perhaps the only band whose success was not tied to these types of lyrics; instead; Los Violadores produced music with a more traditional heavy metal lyrical content.

8. 'Fighting for metal' (t/n).
9. 'One more step in the battle' (t/n).
10. 'The End of the Iniquitous' (t/n).
11. For more information visit https://www.basilio.org.ar. Accessed 11 February 2020.
12. 'Voy a enloquecer/No enloqueceré': I Will Go Crazy/I Will Not Go Crazy (t/n).
13. 'The Great Whore' (t/n).
14. 'Blind Ambition' (t/n).
15. 'The Inquisitor's Living Sustenance' (t/n).
16. 'Before the Old Kings' (t/n).
17. 'Blind Queen' (t/n).
18. 'Tragic Century' (t/n).
19. 'The Industry of Power' (t/n).
20. Among them, the most important one for the purposes of this analysis is the one titled 'Taiwán'.
21. 'From the West' (t/n).
22. 'Outcast' (t/n).
23. It must be stated that, except for *Marginado*, whose authorship is shared with Zamarbide and Cenci, and *No te rindas*, shared with Zamarbide, the rest of the album is exclusively authored by Miguel Roldán.
24. 'Come Towards Eternity' (t/n).
25. 'Don't Give Up' (t/n).
26. 'Resist unto Death' (t/n).
27. 'The Last Battle' (t/n).
28. 'In the Violent City' (t/n).
29. 'Mutant Generation' (t/n).

4

Walkabout, Just Walking about for the Sake of Walking: The Journey as an Ethos in the Poetics of Ricardo Iorio

Manuel Bernal and Diego Caballero

Viajero inmortal,
surcando territorio argentino,
pensando en llegar,
allí esperando están sus amigos.
Viajero inmortal,
la eternidad será su destino.

('Perro Salvaje', Jauría 2013[1])

The name Ricardo Iorio is intricately and popularly linked to heavy metal in Argentina. For years now, scholars have approached heavy metal as an object worthy of study (Calvo 2014), and the poetics of Ricardo Iorio have been of particular interest to this field (Scaricaciottoli 2012). This chapter looks to add to this ongoing analysis. With this goal in mind, we will deploy the concept of *ethos* as the chapter's guiding principle, and, through the use of this idea, engage in a multifaceted analysis of the oeuvre of Almafuerte's frontman.

Influenced by the works of Maingueneau (1999, 2002) and Amossy (1999), we will speak of *ethos* as a double, or stand-in, mirror image of the enunciating subject, who will deploy said image in the act of discourse. The self-referential character that dominates the stylistic choices in Ricardo Iorio's work[2] invites us to delve into his lyrics in order to discover and account for the self-image revealed by the artist in his lyrical output.

Another element that we will approach in this chapter is Iorio's play on the mythical construction of the nation's countryside as a site where the mythology of the origin of the Nation – as established by 'gauchesca' literature and poetics – is on full display (Díaz 2006). In this manner we will showcase the ways in which Almafuerte's frontman constructed his identity (Hall 2003) as an artist, wherein the trope of the journey occupies a pivotal space. Combining the notion of *ethos* with an analysis of the artist's poetics gives us the basis to argue that this constructed identity forms part of the larger mythology that is Iorio, the artist.

Wheels of Metal

The journey is a recurrent topic in the artists and cultural artifacts known to have directly influenced, that is, served as conditions of production[3] of (Verón 1998), Ricardo Iorio's poetics. On the one hand, we find that within rock music the journey serves as a distinctive element of the genre, establishing a poetics of its own. It is beyond the scope of this chapter to establish an exhaustive timeline of the origins of the journey trope in rock music; for now it should suffice to say that, at least in Argentina, the journey as a guiding principle is found in its very origins, particularly in the song 'La Balsa'[4] by Los Gatos (1967). Starting with that initial production – which would later receive a retort from Luis Alberto Spinetta and his song 'Cantata de Puentes Amarillos' (*Artaud*, Pescado Rabioso, 1973) – rock music has showcased the journey as a central theme in a plethora of productions considered representative of the genre. From 'La Casa con 10 Pinos'[5] (*Manal*, Manal 1970) to 'Rutas Argentinas'[6] (*Almendra II*, Almendra 1970), travel, searching, and other forms of movement (in both metaphorical and literal senses) are revisited in the lyrics of Argentinean rock. The emergence of heavy metal in the eighties brought with it the rise of a new figure, the biker, and a new theater of the spectacle, the highway, the latter serving as the location for many of the stories narrated in the songs of the band Riff (Blanco and Scaricaciottoli 2014).

Among the works and artists that make up the conditions of production of Iorio's oeuvre, we also find representatives of the nation's traditional folk music. We would argue that folk music is one of Iorio's influences not just from a strictly musical standpoint, but from a songwriting perspective given the way he articulates his lyrics. Iorio goes so far as to incorporate certain characteristics intricately linked to the aforementioned artistic field.[7] The figure of Atahualpa Yupanqui is presented as the epitome of the wandering artist. The book *Este Largo Camino*[8] (Atahualpa Yupanqui 2008) compiles various texts that give an account of Yupanqui's character as an artist who centers his aesthetic search in the journey, either as a source of contact with 'true' folklore or as something for its own sake, in other words, the journey for the journey's sake.

José Larralde, a classic folk artist who is cited and honored by Iorio as an important influence, can also be included among the musicians who adopted the journey as an important trait in their work: 'at the crossroad/fate will find me/ chewing on my soul' state the lyrics of 'De los Pagos del Tiempo',[9] a song adapted by Almafuerte on its first record (*Mundo Guanaco*, Almafuerte 1995). Similarly, we must also cite gauchesque literature's magnum opus, *Martín Fierro* by José Hernández – a poem predicated on its protagonist's journey which has become an ineluctable reference signaling the tradition of gauchesque poetics - as yet another influence.

The Meanings of the Journey in the Oeuvre of Ricardo Iorio

As we mentioned before, the term *journey* is polysemic; therefore, it is necessary that we go through its various meanings. This proposed approach responds more to what we have observed after going over Iorio's work than to an *a priori* assumption established by the work itself, be it as a desired or an undesired effect. We are talking about possible roads, lateral routes, and shortcuts that weave together and join amongst themselves, seeking to give an account of the continuities that propelled this work.

Flight and Escapism: The Evasion

Raw and unvarnished descriptions of his surrounding reality have remained a constant in the songwriting choices of Ricardo Iorio. The idea of escape materializes as a response to situations in which institutional and economic oppression emerges as a stubborn and infallible affliction that refuses to go away. In particular, escape is captured by two terms that hold a close relationship to the idea of the journey: flight and escapism. The presence of both is all the more emphatic during two periods in Iorio's trajectory: first, during the Hermética era (1988–93) and, second, during the early days of Almafuerte (1995–98).

Frequently invoked in Iorio's oeuvre, escapism receives a negative connotation throughout, one greatly linked to the idea of evasion; that is, to not taking responsibility for any particular situation. This (in)action ineluctably leads to failure, as captured in songs like 'Zamba de Resurrección' (*Mundo Guanaco*, Almafuerte 1995), where Iorio mentions 'gambling and sinister escapism', and 'Ser humano junto a los míos' (*Almafuerte*, Almafuerte 1998), where he declares 'Children born from those who sang in the past/are just a replica of the same escapism'.

In contrast, the idea of flight reveals some differences when compared to escapism. It offers as its premise the existence of a subject who opts to flee when confronted with a situation of oppression. On the one hand, this situation assumes the subject's subordinate position within the context of said condition; on the other, it grants the subject a leading role in the decision to flee, conferring a high degree of choice and agency. This is a recurring idea in Iorio's work as far as the oppression experimented in urban spaces is concerned. Examples of this theme include the following: 'The twentieth century moves on/and the great city shackles me/to the vice of dawn/with its hand made of ethereal concrete' ('Lucero del Alba', *Del Entorno*, Almafuerte 1996); 'From Friday night, to Sunday afternoon/I was caged like a finch, domesticated into submission/by emissaries of the Law, who found my looks/those of a rugged metalhead, bothersome and aggravating' ('Presa Fácil', *Del Entorno*, Almafuerte 1996).

As far as the first meaning goes, the journey is established as synonymous of a liberating alternative. As a response to the oppression experienced in city life by young metalheads during the first years of the reestablishment of the democratic model, the flight response becomes a space of personal fulfillment and freedom. With this in mind, Iorio writes 'They led their own destinies/down a path the rest of the world avoided/and they could feel themselves to be their own state,/their own authority, their personal God' ('Robó un Auto', *Ácido Argentino*, Hermética 1991). In another song, he notes 'Time went by and, not knowing what became of you, we ran in search for you/I dreamt that you were free under the shining sun and I am certain it came true' ('Atravesando Todo Límite', *Ácido Argentino*, Hermética 1991).

Based on this first approach we can conclude that the journey is presented as a method through which we can reach those places where freedom fights for recognition, especially when the city turns into a space of oppression that constrains and curtails the desire for freedom that characterizes the metalhead spirit, thus becoming a spatial metaphor of that other institutional oppression that forces 'metalhead dreams to be delayed' ('Del Colimba', *Víctimas del Vaciamiento*, Hermética 1994). In turn, Iorio's panoramic descriptions create images, blurry in nature, beyond the focus of any conventional lens, in which natural environments merge with a sense of satisfaction and personal discovery.

Feeling Human in the Company My Own People

Iorio's poetics give the journey trope yet another meaning within his oeuvre, one intricately linked to the notion of friendship. In much of his work, friendship serves as the main motivation behind the need to journey. Here we note that physical encounters – the visual contemplation of the other and the recognition of the other's contemplation in the returned gaze – takes on a tangible weight that no exchange in the digital era can replicate or capture, leading Iorio to express the fact that these encounters find their ways into memory, 'forever etching in my heart that forceful embrace', ('Atravesando Todo Límite', *Ácido Argentino*, Hermética 1991). Starting with 'Atravesando Todo Límite'[10] by Hermética, moving through 'Amistades de Tierra Adentro'[11] (*Del Entorno*, Almafuerte 1997), and ending with 'Pa' Pelusa[12] (*Trillando la Fina*, Almafuerte 2012), Iorio's lyrics give shape to a space (interior, distant) in which we can find the most heartfelt expressions of friendship.

In this sense, we can point to examples in Iorio's work where the journey signifies that physical movement necessary for reconnecting with friends awaiting our return to familiar destinations, thus calling attention to the necessary conditions that would bring about a celebration of the collective presence of one's own people. Take for example the song 'Amistades de terra adentro', which celebrates 'Inland friends/heavy metalheads/that endure more because they are less/iron-made are my brothers' (*Del Entorno*, Almafuerte 1997). Or the song 'Allí en San Juan', which affirms that 'At the break of dawn we will make it to San Juan/good wine will greet us there/Pozo, Mondaca and a thousand other friends joined in celebration' (*Piedra Libre*, Almafuerte 2001). Finally, consider the lyrics to 'Toro y pampa', which sets the stage for a gathering, 'Sunday far away from the city/under the sun celebrating with friends/roasted meat, bread, water, and wine' ('Toro y Pampa', *Toro y Pampa*, Almafuerte 2006).

Similarly, friendship can be read as a chance encounter on a trip initiated for some other reason. The song 'Allá en Tilcara'[13] (*Peso Argento*, Iorio and Cianciarullo 1997) presents the discovery of friendship and brotherhood in the indigenous community that gives refuge to the lyric's protagonist: 'The night found me in Tilcara/surrounded by my Indian friends/and I was happy, enjoying a gratifying experience/as I participated in their solitary resistance'. Companionship, the camaraderie of 'my people', gives shape to the notion of friendship found inhabiting Iorio's work.

We noted earlier that the journey shares a literal relationship with friendship; we seek out encounters with our peers, with our friends. However, we have also found that the term can take on a metaphoric role when it intersects with friendship. This is the case in the following examples: 'Alongside heavy metal, I will forge ahead with my message/I will however waver if you are not in the journey with me' ('Vientos de Poder', *Ácido Argentino*, Hermética 1991); 'Towards the other side you and I will journey on' ('A Vos Amigo', *A Fondo Blanco*, Almafuerte 1999). This way the meanings attached to the journey become amplified, given that, to the literal meaning of traveling to meet friends, we must add the metaphoric meaning of the journey as a forward march, a motion towards living life next to those we cherish.

The Journey as an Artistic Odyssey

Allusions that link traveling to heavy metal concerts are more than recurrent. In the song 'Ayer Deseo, Hoy Realidad'[14] by Hermética (*Víctimas del Vaciamiento* 1994), Iorio presents the theme of the journey as a way to fulfill his commitments as a rock performer. He sings 'Going on the road/to bring you a live concert/ennobles my life/fulfills what has always been my dream'. We would argue that 'the road' and 'the concert' turn into the places where Iorio explicitly states what he wishes to build as his own identity. On the topic of identities, sociologist Stuart Hall asserts that 'identities [...] are built within the act of representation, never outside of it' (2003: 18). By painting a clear picture of what we will call his 'meant-to-be' outlook, that is, by creating a metaphor of what he sees as his destiny, Iorio chooses, through his lyrics, the way he wishes to build his image, what exactly he will show of himself in the process, and ultimately how he wishes to be seen.

In Iorio's artistic life, and more precisely in the above mentioned song, Greater Buenos Aires serves as the 'starting point' from which the musician – always in the position of the subjective 'I' – will set out on a journey to various destinations of the erroneously named 'The Provinces'. This is true in the following lines: 'When far from the capital city/the horizons see me/I must march ahead on these roads/and show I am who I wish to be'; 'You won't find me in the concrete rats nest/I'll be burning fuel on deserted highways' ('Deja de Robar', *Hermética*, Hermética 1989).

Upon accepting the notion that identity is built inside of discourse, we must also keep in mind that discourse itself is produced within socio-historical contexts and within particular practices. In the two previously cited songs, the journey adopts the form of travel of the musical work that presents differences with the 'meant-to-be' posed by the song 'Del Camionero'[15] (*Ácido Argentino*, Hermética 1991). 'Driving a truck/I feel fortunate that I live this dream/to which I have given my life/as my father did before me/In it I find my happiness/I need nothing more/that's why I sing what I feel/while riding on a truck'. In the lyrics Iorio opts to mention the profession he inherited from his father (they both worked at some point at the Central Market) and, at the same time, he reinforces the idea that his identity hinges on his relationship with a vehicle. 'I think of the many who will cherish my song/recognizing how they feel as they ride a truck/living the same dream I live', he asserts in the same song.

On a different front, the problems found during travel – again from the perspective of the subjective 'I' assumed by the song's protagonist – serve as another trait that can be located in Iorio's poetics, as is evinced in the following lines:

> Shifting into third gear we head towards death
> to fulfill Almafuerte's commitments
> Things always take a turn

sometimes we hit the mud
other times rock
I only think of getting there
for I know my friends are waiting
I must not delay
I must fulfill my destiny, and I will.
('Pensando en Llegar', *Toro y Pampa*,
Almafuerte 2006)

Thus, the road represents an obstacle, inevitable as it is, that must be faced.

Iorio's move from 'the city that has seen [him] flourish' ('Con Rumbo al Abra', *Ultimando*, Almafuerte 2004) to the countryside of Coronel Suárez (a province in Buenos Aires) brought with it a renewed investment of the journey trope in his lyrics. In the case analyzed above, travel fulfills a pragmatic goal: that is, to reach the point of arrival. In this sense we would assert that 'identities serve as points of temporary connection with the subjective positions that shape us within discursive practices' (Hall 2003: 20). Following Hall's analysis, identities represent positions which the subject is forced to assume; however, the subject simultaneously recognizes these representations as originating from a 'lack'. That is why the city ceases to be the starting point – as stated above – from which Iorio sets out on his journeys starting in 2001; rather, at the time, the southern region of the Buenos Aires province takes on this roll, having a dominant presence in his subsequent work. An initial instance of this new dominant, though not explicit, can be observed in the record *Piedra Libre,* particularly in the song 'Regresando', when he writes: 'I return/to where my bones sleep/the sun slaps me/jolting my plexus' ('Regresando', *Piedra Libre*, Almafuerte 2001). The excessive mileage the musician has to travel to meet with his band mates becomes part of the intricate assemblage that forms and influences his own identity. Similarly, the journey as return trope can also be found in the song 'Trillando la Fina'[16] (*Trillando la Fina*, Almafuerte 2012) where he notes, 'it is over, nothing left but to return/fed up with bunks and dust clouds, I return dragging the sluggish machinery'.

Nonetheless, the array of references to country life and the recurrence of allusion to movement from and within the southern region of Buenos Aires province allows us to assert (at the risk of engaging in the act of psychologizing) that this change in the artist's life had a direct impact on his work. Take, for example, the following example: 'Bonaerense[17] route 76/I sing to you/As you wait for me/For through you I must journey in order to reach/that mountainous corner that harbors national pride' ('Ruta 76', *Ultimando*, Almafuerte 2004). The journey into open land is presented in stark contrast to life in the city. Thus, Iorio writes,

Journeying into the open
as the sun sets
on this goddamned bitch of a life
I await under Tres Picos[18]
for you to finally decide
to run away from the city
that has seen you flourish
run away from those who, defeated, dream you up.
('Con Rumbo al Abra', *Ultimando*, Almafuerte 2004)

In the above passage and elsewhere, Iorio exhibits a need to highlight dichotomies: city/country, center/periphery, homeland/foreign land. Here we must again invoke Stuart Hall, who adds that 'identities are built through the encounter of differences, not at its margins' (2003: 18). As noted in an earlier chapter, the subject needs to encounter that which is not itself, its 'constitutive exterior', in order to define itself. Thus, the lyrics similarly depend on a literary 'exterior', the latter becoming a border where identity can be defined but which also serves as a limit point to the very identity being constructed.

Beyond All Limits

Up to this point we have analyzed the different forms 'the journey' takes on in Iorio's work. Nonetheless, there is another dimension in his work that is important to point out: it is not just the physical body as representation that travels, but his songs (his lyrics) that do so as well. The following selection should serve as evidence of this aspect: 'From Pacheco to Paternal/from Dock Sud to Tres de Febrero/a thousand friends, their hearts open/await this song' ('Gil Trabajador', *Ácido Argentino*, Hermética 1991); 'On this land that stretches from the Atlantic to the Andes/from verdant Chaco to the Fueguinian tundra/lie the crazy dreams/of an Argentine gringo' ('Moraleja', *Víctimas del Vaciamiento*, Hermética 1994). The lyrics travel, fulfilling a distinct poetic function, consequently establishing a metonymic relationship of contiguity which captures the physical presence of the musician. This relationship is complemented by the presence of the music itself, which shaped into song form becomes manifest as well, as is the case in the following lines: 'Gods of the abyss/will save my mark/For themselves, or for those/like you and us three/who, traveling in sound,/dreamt our dreams yesterday and fulfilled them today' ('Mano Brava', *Almafuerte*, Almafuerte 1998). In this last example, the journey of the sound itself enacts, as its primary objective, Iorio's 'meant-to-be' dominant as the artist imagined it.

The Joy of Traveling or the Journey for the Journey's Sake

Far from using as evidence the famous song popularized by Pipo Pescador[19] in which the author notes that 'traveling is a pleasurable endeavor which usually takes us by surprise', we would like to call attention to another distinctive trait in Iorio's oeuvre as far as the representation of the journey is concerned: we would argue that the singer-songwriter leaves clear breadcrumbs throughout his work regarding his fascination with traveling for the sake of traveling. This stylistic trait is a salient characteristic found in Atahualpa Yupanqui's work; after all, for *Yupanqui* the road carries a central role, as evinced in a song like 'A Que le LLaman Distancia', where he sings,

> What strange things we find in life!
> We land where we want to be,
> often without any premeditation
> If the roads are but miles
> on land and nothing else
> what exactly do they mean by 'distance?'
> Please explain it to me somehow.
> ('A Qué le Llaman Distancia', *Volumen 8*,
> Atahualpa Yupanqui 1960)

The same trait finds its way into Iorio's songwriting, which can be noted starting with Almafuerte's 'A Fondo Blanco': 'Crossing the broad plains, to arrive/nowhere fast, just like the wind [...] Aimlessly I journey forward/walkabout, just walking about for the sake of walking/Living my life full speed, never thinking/of coming back or stopping' ('Convide Rutero', *A Fondo Blanco*, Almafuerte 1999).

In examples like these the journey is devoid of the pragmatic purpose of travel; instead, the journey becomes an endeavor done for its own sake. The journey (in this particular rhetorical turn) is no longer representative of the tension between city-country, country-city as was developed earlier. Pleasure sparks the situation, and the metaphor of the road summoning the author serves as a mere excuse to turn on the ignition and travel for no apparent reason other than to travel. In one song Iorio sings 'Heading anywhere/I dream of heading off again/Heading anywhere,/I depart this place/if I forget something/Keep it to yourselves/My pleasure is to lose myself/on the Argentinean roads. I know' ('Allí en San Juan', *Piedra Libre*, Almafuerte 2001). This stylistic trait becomes further expanded in Almafuerte's last record with the following forceful affirmation: 'I am still alive/ still walking about for the sake of walking' ('Pa'l Recuerdo', *Trillando la Fina*, Almafuerte 2012).

'The Time Has Come to Retire'[20]

According to Amossy (1999), any speech act demands the creation of an image of oneself, a representation of the speaking person. It is with a similar notion in mind that Hall posits the idea that it is in representations where identities must be sought (therein lies the relevance of the Jauria citation that opens this chapter). To the meanings already attached to the journey as found in Iorio's work – as a recurrent topic, as a polysemic metaphor – we bring to light on last meaning, with a significance of its own: the journey for its own sake. Based on recurrence, we can mention that the journey takes on a growing importance the more we move ahead chronologically in Iorio's work; the same is the case when it comes to the meanings of the journey itself, which also develops more density and complexity in its form.

The destinations (both physical and symbolic) incorporated by Iorio in his lyrics lead us to posit that, in that extensive and spacious inner territory of the country, magnified by his hours of distant roaming, the leader of Almafuerte has found a kernel of authenticity, which complements and provides meaning to his identity. If at first distance signified a kind of freedom that countered the city's oppression or the possibility of fulfilling his destiny as an artist, over time friendship, in its purest sense, is added, a realization that enables Iorio to find himself. This is clearly the case in the following lines: 'My heart feels full of life as it resists the open country/the fiercest storm and the force of the winds/I want to learn to be/face to face with nothingness/in order to win' ('Vencer el Tiempo', *Toro y Pampa*, Almafuerte 2006). At this point we have reason to assert that Iorio appropriates those traits from gauchesque literature which have been associated to the 'interior' of our country, where the 'pure', the 'original', the 'authentic' become part and parcel of the mythology of origin of our Nation. The fact that there is never an allusion to destinations beyond the geographic limits of our country in his lyrics, we believe, strengthens our argument.

While we consider the topic of the journey fundamental to the history of rock music in our country, the journey as an end in itself becomes crucial to Iorio's work and propels his existence, thus congealing into his *ethos*[21], that is, as the image of the artist himself as revealed in his lyrics. The vastness and complexity of his lyrics build an identity (again, as developed by Stuart Hall) which is dynamic, in turn positioning his traveler persona as a distinctive trait in his work. As we reach the end of the road, we must note that we have opted for just one – full of traces, of signs left to decipher – among many available roads. In the traveler's yearning for more miles to trek, many more await to be traversed.

REFERENCES

Almendra (1970), *Almendra II*, Vinilo, Argentina: RCA.

Almafuerte (1995), *Mundo Guanaco*, CD, Argentina: DBN.

——— (1996), *Del Entorno*, CD, Argentina: DBN.

——— (1998), *Almafuerte*, CD, Argentina: Interdisc.

——— (1999), *A Fondo Blanco*, CD, Argentina: Interdisc.

——— (2001), *Piedra Libre*, CD, Argentina: Interdisc.

——— (2003), *Ultimando*, CD, Argentina: Dejesu.

——— (2006), *Toro y Pampa*, CD, Argentina: Dejesu.

——— (2012), *Trillando la Fina*, CD, Argentina: Dejesu.

Amossy, Ruth (1999), *Images de Soi Dans le Discours. La Construction del Ethos*, París: Delachaux et Niestlé.

Blanco, Oscar and Scaricaciottoli, Emiliano (2014), *Las Letras de Rock en Argentina. De La Caída de la Dictadura a la Crisis de la Democracia 1983–2001*, Buenos Aires: Colihue.

Calvo, Manuela (2014), 'Diálogos que construyen un modo de nacionalismo argentino en el metal pesado argento de Almafuerte', in M. C. Dalmagro and A. Parfeniuk (eds), *Encuentros, Tránsitos y Desplazamientos. Culturas y Literaturas en Tensión y en Diálogo (II)*, Collection --Lecturas del Mundo, Facultad de Lenguas, UNC, Córdoba: Buena Vista Editores, pp. 120–37.

Díaz, Claudio (2006), 'Las Disputas por la Apropiación del Gaucho y la Emergencia del "Folklore" en la Cultura de Masas', lecture before the JALLA, Bogotá, Mimeo, https://www.scribd.com/document/56611137/DiazClaudio. Accessed 11 February 2020.

Hall, Stuart (2003), 'Introducción. ¿Quién necesita identidad?', in S. Hall and P. du Gay (eds), *Cuestiones de Identidad Cultural*, Buenos Aires: Amorrortu, pp. 13–39.

Hermética (1989), *Hermética*, CD, Argentina: Radio Trípoli.

——— (1991), *Ácido Argentino*, CD, Argentina: Radio Trípoli.

——— (1994), *Víctimas del Vaciamiento*, CD, Argentina: Radio Trípoli.

Los Gatos (1967), *Los Gatos*, Vinilo, Argentina: RCA.

Maingueneau, Dominique (1999), 'Ethos, Scénographie, Incorporation', in R. Amossy (dir.), *Images de Soi dan le Discorus. La Construction de l´Ethos*, París: Delachaux et Nietslé, pp. 75–100.

——— (2002), 'Problémes d´Ethos', *Pratiques: Linguistique, Littérature, Didactique*, 113&114, pp. 55–67.

Manal (1970), *Manal*, Vinilo, Argentina: Mandioca.

Pescado Rabioso (1973), *Artaud*, Vinilo, Argentina: Talent/Microfón.

Scaricaciottoli, Emiliano (2012), 'Linajes y rupturas de una imaginación humanista', in M. Vitagliano (ed.), *Boedo. Políticas del Realismo*, Buenos Aires: Título, pp. 53–75.

Verón, Eliseo (1998), *La Semiosis Social*, México: Gedisa.

Yupanqui, Atahualpa (1960), *A qué le Llaman Distancia,* Volumen 8, Vinilo, Argentina: ODEON.

——— (2008), *Este Largo Camino*, Buenos Aires: Cántaro.

NOTES

1. Immortal traveller,/traversing Argentinean territory,/thinking of making it,/to where his friends await./Immortal traveller,/eternity will be your fate (t/n).
2. For further reading, see 'The passion and the ethics: a place for word and tradition in the lyrics of Ricardo Iorio', by Juan Ignacio Pisano, included in this book.
3. Conditions of production refers to a concept developed by Eliseo Verón which calls attention to the ideological influences that give rise to any discourse. For Verón, any discourse is the product of its surrounding economic, social, and political conditions.
4. 'The raft': A song by Los Gatos that narrates the decision of a man to build a raft and travel away, even if it leads towards certain madness and ruin, in search of what he needs (t/n).
5. 'The house with 10 pine-trees' (t/n).
6. 'Argentinean Highways' (t/n).
7. For further reading on this topic, we again refer to the article by Juan Ignacio Pisano, included in this book.
8. 'This Long Road' (t/n).
9. 'Of the Lands of Time' (t/n).
10. 'Beyond All Limit' (t/n).
11. 'Inland Friendships' (t/n).
12. 'For Pelusa' (t/n).
13. 'There in Tilcara' (t/n).
14. 'Yesterday a Wish, Today a Reality' (t/n).
15. 'Trucker' (t/n).
16. 'Threshing the Grain' (t/n).
17. Demonym used to speak about the inhabitants of Buenos Aires Province (t/n).
18. Highest peak of the Sierra de la Ventana mountain range in the province of Buenos Aires (t/n).
19. Popular Argentinean singer/songwriter of children songs (t/n).
20. The original title of this section is 'Ya nos vamos arrimando a la tranquera', an expression with a rural inflection that means that the subject is about to leave the premises, to finish, to end.
21. In the cited works *ethos* is used to account for the political discourse.

5

Passion and Ethics: A Space for Voice and Tradition in Iorio's Lyrics

Juan Ignacio Pisano

Nuestro principal motor son las letras[1]

(Ricardo Iorio)

An Ethics of Language

At the beginning of the song 'Almafuerte', Ricardo Iorio belts out the following: 'Accompanied by what I say, I go'. That syntagma– that smallest unit of discourse – captures a central element in Iorio's lyrics: in the act of the utterance, in the use of words and voice, the author establishes the study of a subject facing the world as the ethical nucleus of his work. The words, penned in order to be sung, are presented as both weapon and shield, as opening aperture and retreat. Giorgio Agamben affirms that human beings are 'living beings in whose tongue their own lives are at stake'; as a result, man 'is that living subject who, in order to speak, must say I; in other words, he must control the word, possess it, and make it his own' (2010: 110). This way of envisioning the relationship between humans, words, and things, lies at the root of Iorio's poetics: somewhere between the collective and the individual, we encounter the freedom contained in the lyrics. The enunciative first person (he who, by speaking, acts) finds his own space and place through the use he makes of said poetics. As if reacting by assuming a position from which he is capable of examining reality, the Iorian subject works to avoid the disintegration of meaning. Agamben's words in *The Sacrament of Language* help us define what the Iorian subject is specifically reacting to: 'When the ethical nexus [...] that binds words, things, and human actions breaks, one becomes witness to the spectacular proliferation of empty words'.[2] Brought together under his singular voice, the author's words work to reconnect this ethical nexus.

To that effect, at one point in the documentary *La H No Murió*,[3] Iorio's bandmates explain how, during the recording process, he would make Claudio O'Connor repeat over and over again the parts in which the words the latter sung were deemed incomprehensible. The lyrical message had to be crystal clear so as to avoid confusion and to guarantee that the enunciating subject's message would be comprehensible to the listener. Consequently, the ethical subject inhabiting the lyric manifests a desire to be as transparent as possible regarding the message being communicated. Ethics,[4]according to Michel Foucault, is not comprised by a pattern of rules to be followed. Rather, ethics is an attitude assumed when confronted with the codes those rules establish; a way of living defined by the subject, who, in turn, constructs a moral subject through the deployment of methodologies grounded in the self. With this in mind, we are interested in genealogizing an ethics which will help us understand the use of language in the creation of lyrics: What do we say? How do we say it? Which fields of knowledge are coming into contact with that which is being said? The relation Iorio establishes with language in his lyrical work takes on a tonality that aligns him with the folk singer and with that paradigmatic text of Gauchesca,[5] *Martín Fierro*, particularly regarding the importance the latter grants to the expression of song. As we will see in this first section, the manner in which Iorio taps into this heritage will produce two lyrical effects: on the one hand, his writing will move from a focus on urban geography and rural cartographic desires to an emphasis in rurality as a vital force; on the other hand, a dissident attitude will mix with a rigid nationalist bent. At the same time, we will analyze the forms passion, or *pathos*, assumed in his work. At the intersection between the rock tradition, heavy metal, and the folkloric form; between dissidence and the conservatism of an unyielding identity; between passion and ethics, lies the focus of the present study.

The Territory of Writing

> *¿Qué somos en este tiempo que es el nuestro?*[6]
>
> (Michel Foucault)

The album *Hermética* offers an ideal starting point for our proposed analytic trajectory. In the opening song, 'Cráneo Candente',[7] we find the establishment of patterns that will greatly influence Iorio's writing: references to the interior of the country, encapsulated under the *pampa* banner; the historical mention of the gaucho; the emergence of the Indian; and, ultimately, the establishment of a historical subtext guiding those lyrics: 'My skull burns under the sun,/as it seeks to comprehend,/while the specters of past/kept my mind awake'. There is a pattern in this first period of Hermética: a reassessment of the historical archive and the subsequent denouncement of a past where we find the motive or origin of the ailment[8] that afflicts the Argentinean present. However, this observational stance in Iorio's writing will not remain the dominant for long: as we travel through his oeuvre, the will to record, to capture (which reaches its definitive form in Almafuerte's last record) will gradually transform into a will to live. His oeuvre will move from the longed-for journey[9] ('Robó un Auto') to the actual journey ('Mamuil Mapu'), from fictional imaginings (the envisioning of the Pampa as a destination) to actual lived experiences (including his own life and his own experiences in the country). That tension between what is recorded and captured and what is lived and experienced becomes his compositional directive.

In the act of recording, the singing voice will invoke three elements that will remain *master-signifiers* (these will not be the only ones) throughout Iorio's oeuvre: 'gaucho', 'indio',[10] and 'pampa'. In 'Cráneo Candente', the voice identifies with the gaucho because it claims to experience the exile 'of the native man' who finds himself under the effects of 'conquering magics/which keep disseminating fear/ like they did with the uprooted gauchos in the past'. Magics, here, must be read as signifying artifice and, in line with Iorio's poetics, lies and fiction, masks and simulacra ('Why falsify?', he asks in 'Sé Vos'). The third song in the record is 'Desterrando a los Oscurantistas'.[11] 'Obscurantism' was a term used by members of the Enlightenment in reference to hoarders of knowledge, that is to say, those who prevented its dissemination, cloaking it behind the pretense of impenetrable complexity. Regarding this, Nietzsche notes that 'the key element in the dark art of obscurantism is not that it wants to hinder individual comprehension, but rather that it wants to blot out our image of the world, and, consequently, obscure our idea of existence' (1958: 105). Magic hides its tricks: it is an art dependent on effects. The tone affected by the poetic voice exposes the ways in which the truth has been concealed through the use of procedures, which the history of our region keeps hidden; in effect, it calls for the removal of obscurantists from our territory. History's lack of clarity meets its match in the lyrical transparency with regards to recorded history: the demand directed at O'Connor mentioned above becomes manifest in the texture of what is being said.

This all leads to the next question: what connections can we point to when it comes to the folkloric tradition? Is it possible, on the other hand, to find links, as was proposed earlier, to *Martín Fierro*? In the gauchesca tradition that preceded the publication of this national poem, the use of song to voice truths had been a pattern, perhaps a necessity: he who sings does so for a reason. Iorio's words – shaped by heavy metal but intricately linked to the gauchesca poetics – are, as a result, words that claim possession of some truth, always within some context, always linked to the specificity of the enunciating subject. *Truth*, as a sort of unveiling, opposes obscurantism and its masks; presents the act of composition as its unavoidable destination; and absorbs all other signifiers into itself. It is, perhaps, the most important signifier throughout his entire oeuvre, the one that runs through his engagement with the gaucho, the indio and the pampa. For this reason, 'Cráneo Candente' establishes the subject as someone who observes himself as part of his brothers, whom he sees as 'overwhelmed with miseries/and deprived of all rights/by the white empire' (references to the white empire are constant in this period, sometimes under different names, but always alluding to the west). The ethical subject assembled in the writing – starting with the first Hermética album – is a subject governed by a *will to truth*, related to the past and the present of Argentina. This truth must be clearly stated for the benefit of its listener.

Throughout Iorio's entire body of work, there is a force intent on averting the truth at all costs: this force takes on the form known as escapism. It is mentioned in the song 'Masa anestesiada', also contained in the self-titled album; moreover, it shows up again in Almafuerte's last record.[12] The truth is once again concealed by the actions of those known to hide or disguise, who, consequently, resort to offering the Argentinean subject alternate lines of flight [these have nothing to do with the lines of flight proposed by Deleuze and Guattari (2002); to achieve this effect, they resort to the available resources of mass culture: TV, popular music, gambling, 'shady shopping malls', among others. Escapism is a manifestation of Argentinean reality in a capitalist society that hides, avoids, and produces destruction, shunning 'fraternal love' and investing its energy in the conviction that no other law exists but the one of 'intimate consciousness': that 'impersonal life' of the 'native man' hidden in the layers of history that the lyrics seek to capture and expose in song, which will enable the 'dawning of a new day'.

That will to truth is, perhaps, among the above-mentioned influences, the most important heritage Iorio absorbs as folkloric intertext, particularly when it comes to Larralde's work[13] and *Martín Fierro*. This heritage comes into clear focus when we consider the following lines taken from *Martín Fierro*: 'to voice some truths/ is to commit sin'; 'I shall speak the truth, for I am no one's sycophant'; 'they shall suffer greatly/should they not believe in my truth'. The preceding lines establish truthfulness as a basic strategy of the poem and, by extension, as a fundamental choice adopted in the type of singing practiced by both gauchesca singers and Iorio. The tradition Iorio retrieves from folklore and *Martín Fierro* is, thus, that of the subject who, in his song, brings forth a truth, that is, he uncovers it.[14]

The most rigidly identitarian modality contained in Iorio's work can be found in songs like 'Orgullo Argentino',[15] 'Cumpliendo mi Destino',[16] and in his interpretation of the figure of Seineldín,[17] among others, which appear to build an essentialist imagining of the Argentinean subject. It is here where the signifier[18]

'Argentinean' represents a subject who stands apart from the rest (from other possible identity signifiers), defining identity according to that which excludes: it is as if, upon affirming his national subjectivity, Iorio moves to leave out all the elements that threaten to contaminate that subjectivity. This stance carries the risk of defining nationalism as an ontological position, primarily because it promotes a rigid identity. The will to denounce falsities – that original tendency towards seeking the truth – is inhibited once one adopts an identitarian orientation. If, as stated above, the Foucauldian ethical subject is born out of the way it interacts with codes, one particular code seems to predominate over the subject's will to truth in the fragments we have taken from Iorio's work: the process of subjectivation changes the source from which it takes its inspiration. A type of moral code associated with the Argentinean subject (in truth, just as arbitrary as any other code) overrules everything else, setting the pattern Iorio will follow in his subsequent writing. Therein lies the risk of this option, of this aesthetic choice. In order to pinpoint these fluctuations, that is, the various paths traversed within his lyrical work, it becomes necessary to submerge oneself in pure *pathos*: that is, in what Ricardo Iorio comes to define as passion.

Passion, Truth

Michel Foucault has written about the existence, within the Greek tradition, of a modality wherein a subject demonstrates the will to speak truth in spite of the risks he assumes in doing so. This modality is known as *parrhesia*. The parrhesiast stands in contrast to the prophet because he does not propose a destination; from the sage, because he does not speak on behalf of wisdom; and from the professor because he does not 'speak, on behalf of tradition, about *tekhne* [...]; [instead,] the parrhesiast puts into circulation the truthful discourse of that which the Greeks called *ethos*' (2010: 41). Returning to what we stated about ethics, parrhesia could be defined as 'the ethics of truthful speech' (Castro 2011: 147). This ethic, guided by the musical aesthetics found in Iorio's work, shares space with the potent quality of passion. Therefore, just as at the beginning of this text we were guided by one particular phrase – 'Accompanied by what I say, I go' – the same phrase will guide us during this second segment, mainly because in that phrase we are not only able to intuit a peculiar connection with language – a possibility of assuming a stance in the complex relationship between words and objects – but because we can also intuit a sort of drive,[19] that is, a type of gesture that exceeds, in all likelihood, the very excess of poetic language and absorbs it into the most untamed of passions. Consequently, the title of this section calls attention to an inalienable link found in Iorio's poetics: a couplet we call ethics/passion.[20] On the one hand, *ethics* signals a vital inclination and defined attitude; on the other hand, *passion* signals the drives within which the word attains meaning.

The Meanders of Passion

As mentioned earlier, one transformation that occurs in Iorio's work speaks of the relationship with the pampas, which, besides being a topical focus, stands as the destination sought after in the life captured by the lyrics. Toward the later part of his career (particularly in his seminar *The Preparation of the Novel*), Roland Barthes (2005) opened the doors for the triumphant return of the author. One specific idea within that text serves our purposes here: writing, according to Barthes, can be seen as an element that helps guide life. Returning to what was discussed in the previous segment, we can observe a peculiar trajectory at work in Iorio's oeuvre: if in 'Cráneo Candente' or in 'Robó un Auto'[21] the pampas represented a destination desired by the singing voice or its characters – either as a chance for reassessment or simply because it represented the final stop in a journey – in songs like 'Toro y Pampa',[22] 'Glifosateando',[23] 'Trillando la Fina', 'Mamuil Mapú', or 'Pa'l Recuerdo'[24] the same voice now views itself as an intricate part of that previously longed-for destination. Life and writing appear to be enmeshed not just because the lyrics capture the lived experiences of the subject-author, but, moreover, because the enunciating subject has been transformed. The group Tiqqun[25] points out that one way of life is a *clinamen* and a reciprocal tendency: that toward which life gravitates, also gravitates towards life. Iorio's relationship with the pampas must be understood in that same way. In a conversation with Larralde (according to his biographer Torres), Iorio expresses surprise at Larralde finding life in the country to be a tedium. However, Iorio reflects and adds: you feel that way because you lived there as a child, and, consequently, became spoiled. That is precisely Iorio's vision: given that Iorio did not live there as a youth but, instead, imagined it, willed it in his poetic language, desired it and wrote about it, life in the country, imagined throughout his writing, became his *clinamen*. Life and work appear inevitable intertwined, accompanied by the will to truth: this triad merges with the homeland and its territory as spaces of passion. As a parrhesiast, he has assumed the risk of enunciating the truth through his own flesh. But that same truth, once it gets enmeshed in the passion for a code (say, a code guiding the perception of the ideal Argentinean being, or what constitutes a certain Argentinean being[26]), becomes restricted: if it can be found, it can be captured.

But, as it winds through the meanders of passion, that same limit becomes, on occasions, the gateway for new possibilities, mainly because Iorio's brand of nationalism, when it does not fall into essentialist tendencies, offers the chance to problematize the homeland as a socio-economic and cultural space.[27] This is particularly the case in the song 'Glifosateando' but also throughout Almafuerte's last album, *Trillando la Fina*. In the case of 'Gifosateando', the enunciating voice takes on the character of a peon who disperses glyphosate on the fields, knowing full well the harm the herbicide causes. The Nation's territory and the diversity of life inhabiting that territory are presented as 'truths' at stake. In that sense – beyond the accusations (justified on occasions) of nationalism, or perhaps in spite of them, and even possibly because of them – the song's lyrics carry a powerful dissenting potency in their immediacy. Iorio's poetics manage to capture diverse ways of 'native' life from the very first lyrics of Hermética's body of work; he amplifies them, exposing them in the materiality of his lyricism, thus extracting them, fictionally, from the 'Máquina de Picar Carne'.[28] The risk mentioned above is found in what is uttered and what is taken on in the process. This set of traits reveals to us an author who, having put himself on the line throughout his work, in his act of enunciating, has attached himself to a tradition of song seen as an ethical tool within gauchesque literature and Argentinean folklore, offering his voice to that project.

In his song '¿Quién?'[29] José Larralde sings: 'I know I'm flesh and bone/conscience and soul/a people and the sweat/That is all I need/to be a brute who raises his voice/with no motive other than the just cause/of those who refuse to be eaten alive' (*Pa' que Dentre* 1969). The raising of the voice, and the enunciating subject's subsequent unwavering claim to that right, is born out of the possibility of speech. Iorio performs a similar gesture when he states 'I am no doctor of the law'.[30] There is no need for an official diploma; the only thing that allows the development of these poetics is pure *pathos*, the most unquestionable passion expressed in song and which is undertaken as an act of violence that brings about the creation of a new right: the right to simply speak, the right to voice truths simply because one possesses the capacity of producing language out of a living body. Therein lies not just possibility but an entire framework that connects the subject of enunciation to the world, the word to the signified, ethics to the codes that allow this world to turn and continue along, 'with or without (the) reflective awareness' of that raised voice. Thus, we reacquaint ourselves with a passion for the limit, finding in that limit a potentiality that fosters writing, not its restriction.

The same Larralde song states the following in its chorus: 'Who taught me to be a brute?/Who taught me? Who taught me?/The womb that carried me/didn't carry any schools or blackboards/Still they say I was born a boy/because they were missing a pawn on the board'. The dialogue addresses early Iorio: he who conceals, teaches, concealing himself as he teaches. The mother's womb, that biological venue of human development, is not a place of abstraction but, rather, an already defined space: the place that produces the brute; the brute who understands that 'hunger only fattens the exploiter', knowledge that remains inaccessible to the employer and the doctor. An intertextual dialogue is established: while Larralde formulates the question, Iorio seeks its answer (we could mention songs like 'El Pibe Tigre',[31] 'Niño Jefe',[32] 'Otro Día para Ser',[33] and several others as examples of this dialogue). It is precisely the chance of giving an answer to this type of question that worries the Nation's territory (not *the Nation* itself) which 'keeps (the) mind (of the poetic voice) awake'.

In the album *Toro y Pampa* we find some continuity with regards to the topics mentioned earlier. To the topic of the pampas, that territory representative of the truth for the Argentinean subject captured in the poetic register, we must add the 'bull', this last entity not just symbolic of the productivity associated with livestock, but also, and of utmost importance to this analysis, symbolic of the inexhaustible potency for passion. References to the bull are not a novelty in the Argentinean literary canon: after all, we find Martín Fierro explaining that 'I am a bull in my own rodeo/but a greater bull in everyone else's' to refer to his ability with song. Hence, the bull becomes a metaphor of courage, but also of fertility: of the song's productivity within the Argentinean tradition. Before José Hernández deployed it in *El Gaucho Martín Fierro*,[34] another gauchesca poet, Luis Pérez, had employed that same trope. From August to October of 1830, Pérez published a Rosista[35] newspaper titled *El Torito de los Muchachos*[36] (he would later edit another one called *El Toro de Once*[37]). For the newspaper, the bull was a symbol of the fight against Unitarians,[38] (symbolically) going out to gore its enemies. As it becomes clear, the bull is a metaphor within the literary tradition Iorio seeks to maintain, making of it an intertextual reference which captures the bravery of voicing, delivering, and singing truths, sustaining these truths with passion. However, that album is of interest here for yet another reason: the song that gives the album its title, *Toro y Pampa*, relays the following message: 'little child from the neighborhood/where I was born/look around you/everyone, everyone is gone/you should leave too'. As stated earlier, the poetic voice has undertaken the journey, and, in turn, it has transformed the singer. The song, while carrying the ethics expressed in its message of encouragement, can also be read as an expression of passion, particularly because the act of moving 'far from the city' is undertaken in the name of 'dispersing',[39] which, in an Iorian turn of phrase, means to give in to one's passions in the space of animality. *Toro* and *Pampa* are the signifiers assigned to the central cores at the end of this poetic discourse. The bull, which appears as an ox in the musicalized version of Pedro Bonifacio Palacios' poem (the poet better known as Almafuerte and from whom the band takes its name) included in *Mundo Guanaco*, is a metaphor of the passionate subject's quality of taking action.

Passion and ethics also come together in another song titled 'Homenaje'.[40] We have already established that Iorio's brand of nationalism carries with it the risk of falling into an identity rigidness. This song in particular, which voices an intense passion for all things Argentinean, will allow us to approach the subject of that risk and problematize it by showing the possibilities inherent within said discourse. Augusto Romero represents 'a living gaucho' who bestows knowledge to the subjective figure at the center of the lyrics. In 'The Narrator' (2001), Walter Benjamin posits that the act of narration testifies to knowledge attained through experience. One who has something to narrate, tradition stipulates, is one who has lived. Like Iorio, or like the subject Iorio constructs in his lyrics, Romero is not a 'doctor of law'; he is a narrator, someone who offers 'wealth', 'profound musings born out of intuition'. Once again, the voice takes over as the central focus: in this singing voice, Iorio recognizes a song that suggests the performativity of speech. In a sense, by opposing those who leave the country in search of 'a guru or something else', Iorio shines a light on and elevates this national 'missing link', this 'living gaucho'.

One could argue that the hard kernel of Iorio's nationalism resurfaces in this revelation. Nevertheless, one could also take a different approach and see this brand of nationalism as the *effect* of a dissenting stance. We are used to seeing nationalism as evil, mainly because of all the catastrophic experiences this school of thought left behind in its wake during the twentieth century. The dangers of nationalism, as a philosophy, rest in the fanatical convictions it can produce, in the ways it can crystalize, that is, harden, an identity. However, by honoring Augusto Romero, Iorio brings to the table another element, another strategy: in a society under the effects of globalization, which forgets the history attached to territories (an idea that since Hermética these lyrics seek to postulate), the subjective voice speaking through these lyrics imagines a being who is not defined by possessing material wealth. Rather, this being is defined by what the subject carries with him as an inalienable property, that is, that thing we call experience, which serves a twofold purpose: it makes him into the person he is, but it also serves as the material he can shape into song form. Is it not possible to see in this turn a stance that goes against conformity? In what can only be seen as a paradoxical turn, the element which, ethically, we initially saw as a reducer of rebellious potential, resurfaces as a passionate attitude that invites dissidence. Consequently, passion, as a blind force, infuses the interstices of the aesthetic choices made throughout the destinations constructed in the lyrics.

Gateway: The Unrelenting Song

Between passion and ethics, or perhaps more specifically, between passion and an ethics defined by its passion for truth, Iorio's lyrics delve into the traditional in order to breathe new life into a type of nationalism that has been concealed thanks to the erasure of the history of the homeland's territory. The lyrics often give this passion the name of 'love', without which, the lyrics seem to argue, it is better to give up. Passion and ethics stand as irreducible poles in a lyrical body of work which, when it manages to not lose itself in a glorification of pride, is able to call for a 'new dawn' of the Argentinean subject. Within that tension, a poetics is built which carries within a question waiting to be answered: what does it mean to be a contemporary singer in a territory, at the heart of a State, in the present moment of a homeland the subject thinks of as his own, an environment he belongs to and which surrounds him? Like oxen, this singer-subject roams, but instead of offering 'bread and stew' to those he sees along the way, he gives out words and music, leaving 'the honorable task of saving the entire world' to 'geniuses and kings'.

The internal logic established in Iorio's relationship to the written word, which was highlighted above in the lyrics for the song 'Almafuerte', finds its culmination in 'Otro Día para Ser', a song which beckons us to 'unmask the irrationality/which has shaped our lives'. However, the song itself also acknowledges that, despite aiding in the unmasking, it will not modify the situation because 'the days will continue to pass/on this inferior planet/as any day, as every day/with or without my reflection'. Nonetheless, the impotence exhibited in the lyrics does not limit the writing work itself, which is defined by the preponderance of work that gives prominence to passion, particularly in the guise of bulls, oxen, and all things animalistic in nature. This is, then, the construction of the self carried out by Iorio as author in all his work, the aporia that defines his trajectory: even if unmasking the irrationality that has shaped all of our lives seems like a lost cause, the lyrics' unrelenting passion, which shapes the act of singing into an act of truth-searching, was, is, and (why not) will continue to be his weapon of choice, that which reconnects the 'ethical nexus' to which we alluded to at the beginning, which brings together words and things under the singular form of an aesthetic. This is the heritage, perhaps unique, undoubtedly distinct, that the words Iorio sings bestow on Argentinean music and culture.

REFERENCES

Agamben, Giorgio (2010), *El Sacramento del Lenguaje*, Buenos Aires: Adriana Hidalgo Editora.

Almafuerte (1995), *Mundo Guanaco*, CD, Argentina: DBN.

——— (1996), *Del Entorno,* CD, Argentina: DBN.

——— (1998), *Almafuerte*, CD, Argentina: Interdisc.

——— (1999), *A Fondo Blanco,* CD, Argentina: Interdisc.

——— (2001), *Piedra Libre*, CD, Argentina: Interdisc.

——— (2003), *Ultimando*, CD, Argentina: Dejesu.

——— (2006), *Toro y Pampa*, CD, Argentina: Dejesu y Tocka Discos.

——— (2012), *Trillando la Fina,* CD, Argentina: Dejesu.

Barthes, Roland (2005), *La Preparación de la Novela. Notas de Cursos y Seminarios en el Collège de France, 1978–1979 y 1979–1980*, Buenos Aires: Siglo Veintiuno Editores.
Benjamin, Walter (2001), *El Narrador, Iluminaciones IV*, Madrid: Taurus.
Castro, Edgardo (2011), *Diccionario Foucault. Temas, Conceptos, y Autores*, Buenos Aires: Siglo XXI Editores.
Deleuze, Gilles and Guattari, Félix (2002), *Mil Mesetas. Capitalismo y Ezquizofrenia*, Madrid: Pre-Textos.
Foucault, Michel (2010), *El Coraje de la Verdad. El Gobierno de Sí* y de los *Otros II*, Buenos Aires: Fondo de Cultura Económica.
Hermética (1989), *Hermética*, CD, Argentina: Radio Trípoli.
——— (1990), *Intérpretes*, CD, Argentina: Radio Trípoli.
——— (1991), Ácido *Argentino*, CD, Argentina: Radio Trípoli.
——— (1994), *Víctimas del Vaciamiento*, CD, Argentina: Radio Trípoli.
Hernández, José (2005), *Martín Fierro*, Buenos Aires: Editorial Norma.
Lacan, Jacques (2014a), *Escritos 1*, Buenos Aires: Siglo XXI Editores.
——— (2014b), *Escritos 2*, Buenos Aires: Siglo XXI Editores.
Larralde, José (1969), *Pa' que Dentre*, LP, Argentina: RCA Victor.
Loreti, Nicanor (2011), *La H No Murió*, Independent Production.
Ludmer, Josefina (2000), *El Género Gauchesco: Un Tratado sobre la Patria*, Buenos Aires: Perfil.
Nietzsche, Friedrich (1958), *Humano, Demasiado Humano*, Buenos Aires: Aguilar.
Pérez, Luis (1978), *El Torito de los Muchachos*, Buenos Aires: Instituto Bibliográfico Antonio Zinny.
Rama, Ángel (1982), *Los Gauchipolíticos Rioplatenses*, Buenos Aires: Centro Editor de América Latina.
Tiqqun (2015), *Introducción a la Guerra Civil*, http://translationcollective.files.wordpress.com/2011/03/introduccion-a-la-guerra-civil.pdf. Accessed 1 August 2015.

NOTES

1. Lyrics are our main engine (t/n).
2. Regarding this examination we can think of songs such as 'La Máquina de Picar Carne', 'Olvídalo y Volverá por Más', 'Memoria de siglos', among others in which the relationship between what is said and what is undertaken is questioned.
3. 'The H is not dead', reference to a popular metalhead chorus which, in their opinion, establishes some continuity to the history of *Hermética* (t/n).
4. The development of the concept here utilized is taken from his seminars (Foucault 2010).
5. Gauchesca represents a literary genre produced in Argentina between the late eighteenth century and early nineteenth, which posits as an authorial prerequisite that the subject that produces it be a literate person who speaks as if he were a gaucho. That is to say, it is not the poetry of gauchos, but a literary artifice. For further reference, see the texts by Josefina Ludmer (2000) and Ángel Rama (1982) cited in the references.

6. *What are we in this period that is our own?* (t/n).
7. 'Burningskull' (t/n).
8. For further understanding of this topic, see Ezequiel Alasia's essay in this volume.
9. For further development of the journey topic in Iorio's lyrics, see Manuel Bernal and Diego Caballero's chapter in this volume.
10. 'Indio' is the Spanish translation of the term Indian when used to refer to Native Americans. In the context of Gauchesca poetics, it has a distinctive, untranslatable semantic connotation, a folkloric tone, that binds it to gaucho and pampa. Lacking an English equivalent, we have opted to leave the original Spanish term (t/n).
11. 'Uprooting the Obscurantists' (t/n).
12. This is the case with 'Muere Monstruo, Muere'. It can also be found in other songs by Almafuerte such as 'Serhumanojunto a los míos' and 'Zamba de resurrection'.
13. José Larralde (1937) is an argentine folkloric singer with a vast work. He is considered one of the most important folkloric singers of the last decade.
14. The lyrics to the song 'Vientos de Poder' ('Forceful Winds', t/n) contain a quote taken from *Martín Fierro* with the distinction that the quoted fragment inverts the enunciating position. Is this an aesthetic gesture or a challenge to the listener? The answer can be found in another core element of his poetics: Iorio will never cease to construct himself, as an artist, from a position of individuality. That is to say, to record the lyrics as he did implies, as an aesthetic gesture, the affirmation that, despite referring to the literary-poetical tradition, he will not do so passively, without modification: instead, he will absorb it and deploy it in his own voice, under his own devises. Therefore, he assumes a paradigm of activity, not of passivity. It is as if the famous dictum 'You are you, I am me' which he repeatedly pronounces in his interviews materializes in the poetic realm; or as if the words in another one of his lyrics, which by now is considered a hymn for Almafuerte's followers, 'Sé Vos' ('Be Yourself', t/n), became flesh.
15. 'Argentinean Pride' (t/n).
16. 'Fulfilling my Destiny' (t/n).
17. Mohamed Alí Seineldín, Argentinean colonel sentenced to life imprisonment for leading several military uprisings during the eighties (t/n).
18. Here, I am referring to Lacan's (2014a, 2014b) use of the term.
19. The original text uses the word 'pulsión' which is a reference to the Freudian concept of the drives (t/n).
20. It is worth recalling, not without irony, that as stated in the song 'Tú eres su Seguridad' ('You Are His Security'; t/n), passion is something that can be suffered.
21. 'He Stole a Car' (t/n).
22. 'Bull and Pampa' (t/n).
23. Neologism we would loosely translated as 'Glyphosating', meaning to disperse glyphosate (t/n).
24. 'In the Name of Memory' (t/n).

25. Tiqqun is the name of a French publication about philosophy, founded in 1999.
26. The Argentinean code seems to be governed by a defense of the national outside of any context; that is why it becomes an essentialism. His defense of Seineldín is perhaps born out of this tendency. That is why, when the defense of all things Argentinean as the ideal moral code overtakes the act of composition, a limit is set up and the debate about what is truly Argentinean loses steam.
27. For more on this subject, see Emiliano Scaricaciottoli's chapter in this volume.
28. 'Meat-Grinding Machine', song by Almafuerte (t/n).
29. 'Who?' (t/n).
30. The same logic can be found in *Martín Fierro*.
31. 'The Tiger Child' (t/n).
32. 'Child Boss' (t/n).
33. 'Another Day of Being' (t/n).
34. 'The Gaucho Martín Fierro' (t/n).
35. 'Rosista': adept to the figure and ideas of Juan Manuel de Rosas, Argentinean military figure and politician who during different periods governed the Province of Buenos Aires and the Argentinean Confederation in the nineteenth century (t/n).
36. 'The Boys' Little Bull' (t/n).
37. 'The Bull From Once' (t/n).
38. 'Unitarios', adepts of the nineteenth-century Unitarian Party in Argentina.
39. 'Esparcimiento' carries various meanings. First, it calls attention to the act of spreading or scattering. This is meant to be seen as scattering seeds, that is, the seeds of passion. But this act of spreading can also be seen as the liberty found by animals roaming free in the Pampas. Finally, and perhaps the principal meaning invoked here by the author, it is meant to paint a picture of giving in to primal instincts. Thus, animality, passions, and freedom all come under this singular word.
40. 'Homage' (t/n).

6

The Reason Behind My Writing: Another Day of Being

Ezequiel Alasia

The Illness

> *Si Bertolt Brecht decía que había que lograr*
> *pensar en la cabeza del otro, nosotros hemos logrado, muchas*
> *veces y mutuamente, escuchar con los oídos del otro.*
>
> (Blanco and Scaricatiottoli 2014)[1]

Pierre Bourdieu (1991) defined the concept of field as a space of action and influence where certain social relationships converge. The position each participant assumes within a field depends on the rules governing it. At the same time, those same fields, once unified through their shared influences and power relations, help define social structures and subjects, defining these as either the dominator or the dominated.

This dominant structure, which is always in constant tension, sets up spaces that make visible and 'semiotize social tensions, cultural conflicts, and policies of domination' (Ugarte and Sanjurjo 2008: 21). Out of these spaces, we witness the emergence of a poetics, which thanks to its own maneuvers, will give rise to actions of resistance, which in turn will go against that which they come to define as 'evil'.

Out of resistance grows a sense of existence, and it is from this perspective that the poetics[2] of heavy metal is presented as a space from which its members can confront 'evil'. Argentinian band Almafuerte makes this idea explicit in their song 'Sé Vos', when they affirm that 'Those who endure, exist' ('Sé Vos', *Almafuerte* 1998). Heavy metal music already possesses a memory embedded in it by the very field it inhabits, and this memory grants it the ability to take a divergent position when confronted with reality; tapping into metaphoric language to explain the way society functions, the metal subject claims that 'I only convey/what I observe' ('En las Calles de Liniers', *Hermética* 1994). These metaphors are not just a figure of speech, but, more importantly, a mechanism that serves to comprehend the world. Illness represents one such set metaphors, a set which Susan Sontag (2003) warns must be deactivated in order to comprehend the world. And it so happens that heavy metal takes on this task of analyzing illness, defining its parameters in order to deconstruct them.

Advanced industrial societies have shown an unwillingness to accept illness as a reality, opting instead for the dissemination of false hope when it comes to the ill. With this in mind, Hermética effectively deconstructs this unwillingness when they sing, 'Don't play hide and seek/because to fear death/is to distort our values' ('Para que No Caigas', *Hermética* 1989). As we will see in this chapter, heavy metal actively engages with the diverse ways in which society and culture seek to define, modify, and control our engagement and understanding of illness, setting the stage with this engagement for spaces where its practitioners can undertake acts of resistance.

Illness as Metaphor

According to Aristotle in his *Poetics* (1974), metaphors consist of giving one thing the name of another. From the outset, we understand the impossibility of thinking without metaphors and that all thought is an act of interpretation. Often, these thoughts are imposed through the creation of a series of social relationships that comprise what in our times we have come to identify as the 'State'. This concept, which Foucault (2006) would have potentially argued is itself a constructed reality,[3] emerges from the diverse relationships that occur within a social setting: these can include government, institutions, and even morals. This framework gives the dominant classes the capacity to regulate people's conduct with the express goal of achieving certain objectives, demanding that its subjects assimilate and reproduce them; thus, the State becomes an instrument that develops in a dynamic fashion, eventually exceeding any bureaucratic and institutional boundaries.

Illness does not solely exist in the poetics of heavy metal; in fact, because of its tense engagement with other fields, it absorbs influences that manifest in other realms, as is the case with literature. Even when the sense imposed by the written word distances itself from the sense imposed by the spoken word (a result of the different production modes), it is impossible to deny that, based on the quotidian, on 'the space where the system's true face is revealed and stripped naked' (Blanco and Scaricaciottoli 2014: 19), both instances end up situated in quasi-similar spaces.

Uprooting the Obscurantists

Illness originates out of the imbalance imposed by the same political language which divides notions such as 'state and society', 'public and private', 'government and market'. This imbalance can be identified by a recognition of the social structure that is imposed through the class struggle. Beatriz Preciado's theorization of illness (Preciado 2013) begins with a consideration of the notion of 'stigmas'. 'Stigmatizations'[4] are generated in order to control society and, by extension, to force its self-regulation, causing each member to reproduce the same concepts levied against his or her own class, an idea captured by the following lines: 'Through the TV they spread their infection/the slaves of the old transgressor' ('Desterrando a los Oscurantistas', *Hermética* 1989). This language of 'illness' grants the State the power to suppress and divide those subjects who do not reproduce the cultural homogeneity they demand, forcing them to organize through categories that are imposed upon them. Heavy metal, however, denounces these imposed divisions by reformulating the parameters of illness to include everyone; in other words, everyone is ill according to the perspective of heavy metal, a sentiment captured in the following lines:

> To be guardians or sentinels of all the honey
> which the despicable powers that be store in every hive
> Predator, ecologist, poor, or great lord
> Drug addict, doctor or patient
> each a member of this lot
> ('Otro Día para Ser', *Hermética* 1994)

Consequently, categorizations and even class divisions break down given that both the dominators as well as the dominated are seen as part of the illness, with the former imposing it and the latter reproducing it: bourgeoisie and proletariat, State and people have a role in the spread of the illness.

Heavy metal poetics approach and build the concept of illness by considering a series of relationships that occur at more complex levels, wherein, without ever thinking of the State per se, each individual actually helps in reproducing it. Take the following lines as examples of this engagement: 'When one least expects it/ the poison is already running through your veins' ('Veneno', La Renga 1996);[5]

> We are one step away from darkness
> a product of the minds that wish to drown us
> in the ruthless swamp of violence.
> Stop and think before you act

whether there is anything to gain from allowing yourself
to be used as a purveyor of dementia
('Solución Suicida', Letal 1984)

One thing of note in these lyrics is the warning to the listener on the part of Letal, an appeal to pause and think, about the subject's positionality as part of a collective: '*We* are' the message states clearly. A nihilistic Ricardo Iorio gives voice to a concrete repudiation of any power relations originating out of 'dementia', out of illness. And the appeal does not stop there: 'Quick, use your strength and defeat/those who, day after day, conceal the light/Planting in you ideas of corruption and pain/of corruption/And pain.../Creators... of your impatience'. As it conceals the truth, the system comes head to head with the nihilistic vision of heavy metal's poetics, a poetics which in turn helps identify the creators of illness, 'the concealers of the light', as the enemy to be eliminated. Furthermore, the song implores the listener to 'Awaken your mind in order to eliminate/the perverse goblin that lies within/charging you with negative forces'. These lines evidence the presence of a conscious author who has almost achieved a mystical state, as he tries to awaken those he sees stuck on the other side. The goblin, that malevolent creature which is often presented as the root of evil in many texts (the goblin in Shakespeare's *A Midsummer Night's Dream*[6] comes to mind), is not presented here as a mythological creature, but, in fact, as a real one.

Illness represents a strategic field of power relationships; in this field different types of behavior are established, for both the rulers and the ruled. Accordingly, literature emerges as a powerful tool which helps reveal the different articulations of subjugation that are reproduced, not only in institutional apparatuses, but also in the subjects engaging with these apparatuses. Inspired by Deleuze and Guattari's development of the notion of 'schizophrenia'[7] as a way to better understand these types of articulations – *schizein* means split and *phren* means mind – we can posit that these apparatuses of control and domination function as mechanisms that promote fragmentation, guiding these minds towards ideas which allow for the continued development of the State's preferred modes of production and existence (Deleuze and Guattari 2009).

The Curse of Artificial Representation

Within heavy metal poetics, the metaphor of illness plays an intricate role in the critical deconstruction of the power relations found in its vicinity. This notion materializes in the following guises:

As the Moral Fiber of the Individual and Society

In *The Magic Mountain*, Thomas Mann (1924) presents a clinic dedicated to the treatment of tuberculosis as a symbol of society. The same occurs in the song 'Hospitalarias Realidades'[8] (Hermética 1994), where the clinic takes on the same value as the one found in Mann's novel: the clinic becomes a representation of reality. These represent two different sets of poetics with distinct sensibilities in terms of their respective aesthetic expressions, yet they share a similar interest in their desire to call attention to the same problem, even if they do so within different battlefields.

In Mann's novel, the character of Naptha voices his opinion that 'whosoever desires to be cured is not looking for anything other than to be dehumanized and get closer to his animalistic side' (2009: 751–52). Even though illness is caused and spread by the human race, metal music holds out the possibility for change (and this change approximates, at some given moments, a return to the animal within the human). There is always a type of exchange taking place within the fields of good and evil. In order to fight, one must organize with others, a sentiment expressed in the following lyrics: 'To those who are fed up with seeing/the faces that symbolize the past/join us, we have a spot for you/in our metal brigade' ('Brigadas Metálicas', *Luchando por el Metal,* V8 1983). The preceding song taps into the 'typical organizational models of the seventies' (Blanco and Scaricaciottoli 2014: 112) and distances itself from the rejection of instinct, instead championing instinct as something unique and liberating. With this in mind, Hermética invites its listeners to 'Kill the fear that holds the animal back/cleanse the body/for in it you exist/If you seek freedom/stop looking for it on the outside/Man of a thousand men be born/be born now' ('Tú Eres Su Seguridad', Hermética 1989). Freedom is found in the cleansed body, in the negation of bourgeois dialectics; a kind of cure and/or armor is proposed as the way to resist the system's virus.

As a Common Metaphor for Moral or Social Decay

Exhibit A:

- 'Reason/awaits your fall./What you concealed/returns to condemn you./I discovered the sham/of your deceit,/I am well aware/that there is so much more' ('La Gran Ramera', V8 1986).
- 'Disaffected renegades in self-denial/lacking calmness and mercy/They fixate on the little girls' triangles to feed their lecherous ways/as they masturbate in solitude' ('En las Calles de Liniers', Hermética 1991).
- 'You can find the people already there/sleeping next to the TV./Their God is the God of indigestion' ('Desde el Oeste', Hermética 1991).

- 'He asked me about the capital/and the things that went on there/and I could only talk/about injustice/and their desire for the fruits/of their own greed' ('Lo Frágil de la Locura', La Renga 1996).

As exhibited in the quotes chosen above, heavy metal inverts the concept of morality – a set of rules defined and imposed through the power relations that take place between religion, institutions, and the State – and applies it to these same organizations; those which, through their discursive practices, subject the people to a defined set of morals through the use of actions which, should they have the capacity of judging themselves in the same fashion in which they judge the proletariat, would be deemed immoral. Decadence is born out of the numbness found in ordinary life, out of the concealment of truth, out of the desire for power, and out of the complicity of those who breed these tendencies within the 'dominated' class. Confronted by an excess of decadence, the bourgeois will seek to restore order; in other words, it will institute mechanisms of repression of their highest order. In response to this bourgeois excess and understanding this excess as immoral, heavy metal will deploy the poetic currents showcased above.

As a Sign Calling for an Individual to Escape Their Fate[9]

Exhibit B:

- 'He stole a car to travel/towards the living solitudes/To feel a part of them/was his most ardent dream' ('Robó un Auto', Hermética 1991).
- 'You won't regret/riding on my steel horse;/with him we go in search of your soul,/you will find it, I am sure' ('Corcel de Acero', Hoy No Es Hoy 1987).
- 'The anarchic motorcyclist subjectivity proposed exhibits a tendency towards flight, towards escape, fleeing away from the system it denounces, an alternate yet parallel modulation of the modern city, not applicable to the country or the rural space but, rather, to that other sign of modernity: the expansive highways...' (Blanco and Scaricaciottoli 2014: 107).

While the quote presented above asserts the presence of a pronounced ideological tendency within the concrete political discussions approached here, it is inevitable to point out that this is not always the case. The journey, or the escape if we prefer to call it so, is a trope used within fourteenth-century western literature to denote an undesirable present condition, an illness that stalks and contaminates the city. The instinct of survival determines the subject's actions; the animal within, not our capacity for reason, governs the subject's decisions. The subject is alerted by a series of factors that naturally drive him towards survival, thus making the escape an instinctive necessity rather than an ideological position.

As a Tool of Redemption for the Ill and Marginalized

Exhibit C:

- 'Had I learned to be an animal from the start/I'd possess a noble instinct instead of this sorrow' ('Cuando Vendrán', La Renga 1996).
- 'Kill the fear that holds the animal back/cleanse the body/for in it you exist' ('Tú Eres Su Seguridad', Hermética 1989).
- 'Stop abusing your animal/for you must not conquer it;/instead, love and preserve it./I'm letting you know before you are/suffocating under the wall' ('Vida Impersonal', Hermética 1989).

Whenever someone is afflicted by an illness, they visit a clinic looking for a cure. In her presentation titled *The Death of the Clinic?*, Beatriz Preciado defines the clinic as an apparatus of social control. The clinical apparatus defines and applies the various stigmas and metaphors (of each particular illness) as a way to control society. How does it achieve this? By easily fragmenting society, in turn making each member complicit in their own self-regulation as each willingly reproduces the laws of the clinic and its categorizations. In the present, those subjects the system defines as ill – subjects who fail at reproducing cultural homogeneity (homosexuals, transexuals, people with AIDS, people with tuberculosis, drug addicts, and other marginalized identities – are organized within categories of control imposed on them. Preciado, in an analysis that aligns her with 'Otro Día para Ser', states that all of these fragmented identities are grouped under the category of 'the dominated'; as a response, she urges these segmented groups to organize beyond the boundaries the system has imposed on them. Well acquainted with this category of 'the dominated', heavy metal will equally propose its adherents to break from it: 'When they bring their impersonal lives/ into their struggles/the Earth will be illuminated' ('Vida Impersonal', Hermética 1989).

As a Way of Highlighting the Awareness of Death

Heavy metal sheds light on matters pertaining to morality and the complexities of a life lived within an infirm system. It will strive to breathe new life into the anesthetized, dogmatized, and lifeless minds of individuals, as it tries to restore these to their natural, animal state. This objective becomes evident in the following fragment:

> Suffocating under the wall
> held up by the lingering shadows
> frozen there as evidence of their revelation.
> Held up by the dead
> still living on the margins.
> Like clouds, they come and go.
> Nourishing the Inner Self,
> witnesses of eternity.
> Incapable of comprehending
> that the time for a new dawn is here
> ('Vida Impersonal', Hermética 1989)

The intention here is to illuminate the dead who remain asleep, those who watch life go by without understanding its true essence. Heavy metal, it would seem, shoulders the heavy pedagogical task of bringing people into a condition of reason through the development and analysis of everyday circumstances. Not only does the new dawn bring light, it also enacts an awakening in a consciousness capable of unveiling the obscurantist mechanisms of domination, something made evident in the following lines:

> A valiant soul is reborn
> intuition revealed it to me,
> he is not Jesus, he is not the Christ,
> nor is he the Devil's son.
> He is the one who will reveal
> what many prefer not to see.
> What many want to conceal,
> what every young person wants to know
> in order to live without fear
> ('Predicción', Hermética 1991)

As we see in this particular case, resurrection (an ability ascribed to Christianity's superhero, but also to Kenny, South Park's beloved character) saves the day, bringing forth from the great beyond 'a valiant soul'. This awakened dead one (the previous song attempted a collective awakening; this song, in turn, awakens only one, a warrior) will be able to live free, thanks in great measure to the armor of consciousness provided by heavy metal; as he lives without fear, he will, at the same time, show how the mechanisms of domination work, how the illness operates within those who prefer not to see, for fear of confronting reality.

As a Strange Force Capable of Penetrating Human Life and Destroying It

Exhibit D:

- 'Native peoples of my homeland/are addicted and confused./By the sinister claws of the great whore/who proudly celebrates five hundred years/of arriving with her Fleet' ('La Revancha de América', Hermética 1991).
- 'The city sleeps during the blackout,/the purge is taking place/and lost in the confusion,/are the drowned screams of my despair' ('Víctimas del Vaciamiento', Hermética 1994).
- 'Letting fear stop them/is like shooting them in the back./They continue to feed the suffocating darkness' ('Yo No lo Haré', Hermética 1989).

The force mentioned here can be equated to pathologies such as HIV and cancer, illnesses that overwhelm the body and reproduce to the point of killing the person. This term appears in the first two songs as a key problem developed by the notoriously 'sinister forces of evil' that V8 often mentioned. The system, with its cultural and social impositions, promotes the adoption of vices on the part of the people, including consumerism, alcoholism, etc., in order to deflect attention away from what matters, thus controlling their ways of life. It is a popular belief that these subjects represent ideal candidates for developing some type of cancer; the illness, they would argue, originates as a consequence of the rupture of the balance between mind and body, a balance assailed and shattered by the State itself. Confusion and fear, repression and the media, stand as key weapons this illness deploys in order to prosper and expand. And it is precisely the lack of resistance which allows for its unchallenged expansion.

The Search for Reason: A Proposed Cure

'Even the disease most fraught with meaning can become just an illness. It happened with leprosy [...] and it is bound to happen with AIDS, when the disease is much better understood and, above all, treatable' (Sontag 2003: 84). Within a heavy metal poetics, understanding an illness more effectively can only occur when people become class conscious. Only the masses can change what the masses suffer. Heavy metal promotes resistance, identifying the enemy and recognizing who reproduce these conditions. As a way to confront this gigantic monster, creator and disseminator of the illness, it proposes the adoption of different methodologies: resistance and conflict, organization and escape. On a personal level, I identify four postulates contained within heavy metal poetics which manifest when a search for a type of cure, a solution to the problem, becomes a pressing matter: on the one hand, destruction and resistance; on the other, escape and purification.

Through destruction, a key concept found in V8's discography which needs no elaboration, an attack is levied on the State, which represents the source of the illness. Destroying the virus simultaneously annihilates the bourgeois state in a sort of revolution imbued with a nihilistic inflection and an Anarcho-Darwinist character. Only the uncontaminated, '[t]hose sick of withstanding/the weeping of the peacemongers' will succeed in this endeavor. Within this first category, we find the resistance: those who avoid becoming ill, those who avoid the infection. This resistance is born from a newfound awareness that identifies the disseminators of the illness, a kind of class consciousness that points to the bourgeois as the enemy. At the same time we have the joining together of a sector, in this case the heavy metal sector, under the banner of 'Brigadas Metálicas', as a key strategy that looks to avoid infection as well as bring about the destruction of dominant institutions.

However, the same nearness established in understanding and reproducing those cures brings with it the predicament of infecting V8 itself. The illness finds its way into the womb of metal's revolutionary core, turning its most faithful standard bearers into a kind of double agent recruited in the service of the illnesses' ideology, of its religion. This switch can be witnessed the moment the band stops promoting 'destruction' and, instead, starts advocating for the avoidance of destruction.[10]

Upon coming to grips with the apparent failure of preceding attempts at a cure, and seeing their chief mentors succumbing to the illness, two new alternatives emerge for the metal subject. First, we identify the option of the escape, an option that is less a search for a numbing escapism than a fleeing from the source of infection, as was defined above in the segment titled 'As a Sign Calling for an Individual to Escape Their Fate'. Those involved seek an isolated space where the illness and its purveyors have no reach or, at the very least, where they lack the same influence they display in their centers of power, that is to say, in the cities. An example of this search is depicted in 'Robó un Auto' where the option of living in solitude will enable the individual to inhabit a space where he can nurture his Being and fulfill his dreams.

In conjunction with the aforementioned escape we find 'the purification' of the body, of the soul. The escaping subject carries with him, in one way or another, certain symptoms of the illness that perhaps have not yet fully developed. This purification, which will be enacted in those moments when the self recognizes itself, will exhibit, unlike previous occasions, a more mystical and more spiritual content. The body, upon shedding its connections to materiality, individualism, and other contaminating factors, will become enlightened as it accepts the benefits of an impersonal life. The attainment of self-awareness and the liberation of the inner animal, unhindered by repression (instincts are no longer neglected, but recognized), will allow the subject to attain a pure state. The animal, a key figure for nihilism as well as heavy metal poetics, will be instrumental in the awakening towards consciousness: to love the inner animal is to save oneself. The act of becoming animal will not only speak of an anti-rationalist philosophy that champions a return to our instinctual tendencies, but it will also be an integral part of a new way of life linked to practices presently aligned to anarcho-primitivism. Consequently, freedom will no longer be located outside the self; instead, it will be seen as an element which is inhibited in us the moment we are born, that which we possess inside and which, because it lies hidden, awaits for an awakening that will allow it to guide us in our search for liberation.

REFERENCES

Almafuerte (1998), *Almafuerte*, CD, Argentina: Interdisc.

Aristóteles ([1457 b 7-25] 1974), *Poética*, Capítulo XXI, Madrid: Gredos.

Blanco, Oscar and Scaricaciottoli, Emiliano (2014), *Las Letras de Rock en Argentina. De la Caída de la Dictadura a la Crisis de la Democracia (1983–2001)*, Buenos Aires: Colihue.

Bourdieu, Pierre (1991), *El Sentido Práctico*, Madrid: Taurus.

Deleuze, Gilles and Guattari, Felix (2009), *El Anti Edipo. Capitalismo y Esquizofrenia*, Barcelona: Paidós.

Foucault, Michel (2006), *Seguridad, Territorio y Población*, México: Fondo de Cultura Económica.

Frith, Simon (1998), *Performing Rites: On the Value of Popular Music*, Boston: Harvard University Press.

Hermética (1989), *Hermética*, CD, Argentina: Radio Trípoli.

——— (1991), Ácido *Argentino*, CD, Argentina: Radio Trípoli.

——— (1994), *Víctimas del Vaciamiento*, CD, Argentina: Radio Trípoli.

La Renga (1996), *Despedazado por Mil Partes*, CD, Argentina: Interdisc.

Letal (1984), *Letal – Demo*, Argentina: Independent.

Mann, Thomas (2009), *La Montaña Mágica, Barcelona:* Bolsillo Edhasa.

Pappo y Hoy No Es Hoy (1987), *Plan Diabólico*, LP, Argentina: Talent.

Preciado, Beatriz (2013), *La Muerte de la Clínica*, Conference by Beatriz Preciado at the Reina Sofía Museum, March, https://www.youtube.com/watch?v=4aRrZZb-FmBs. Accessed 11 February 2020.

Sontag, Susan (2003), *La Enfermedad y sus Metáforas*, Buenos Aires: Taurus.

Ugarte, Mariano and Sanjurjo, Luis (2008), *Emergencia: Cultura,* Música y *Política*, Buenos Aires: CCC.

V8 (1986), *El Fin de los Inicuos*, LP, Argentina: Umbral.

NOTES

1. 'Just as Bertolt Brecht believed that we should think as if we were in another's mind, we have managed, on many occasions, in a collective way, to hear and listen with the ears of the other' (t/n).
2. The word *poetics* 'does not refer to a particular literary genre such as poetry; rather, it has a wider scope that extends to include every literary event' (Blanco and Scaricaciottoli 2014: 15).
3. Foucault, M. (2006), *Seguridad, territorio y población*, Mexico: Fondo de Cultura Económica, p. 136.
4. By stigmatizations, we mean to define the use of metaphors which are imposed by the different power relations (institutions, the State, mass media).
5. 'Genre is a way of assigning music to its now market, or alternatively, a market to its own music [...]. The logic of labelling depends on what the label is for; genre maps change according to who uses them' (Firth 1998: 76–77). We acknowledge that including *La Renga* within an analysis of heavy metal might seem a somewhat forced choice; nevertheless, we believe that this band's work shares the same tensions found in the metal genre.
6. Within English literature these creatures are known as 'Pan', goblins or fauns with goat feet and upper bodies similar to that of a human, whose purpose is to generate conflict and disorient the other characters.
7. For more on this, see Gilles Deleuze and Felix Guattari (2009), *Anti-Oedipus: Capitalism and Schizophrenia*, New York: Penguin Classics.
8. 'Hospital Realities' (t/n).
9. This topic is also analyzed by Bernal and Caballero in the present book.
10. As similar appeal occurs in Psalm 58, where David urges us to 'Not destroy'.

7

Piedra Libre[1]: Referential Tensions in Argentinean Heavy Metal Lyrics Since the Political Crisis of 2001/2002

Emiliano Scaricaciottoli

Estrategias para Evitar el Ablande[2]

Reflejado en la tristeza de la infancia
moría un sueño en cada aventura
mezclado entre inocencia y llanto
creció consumido en su existencia
De grande buscó la respuesta
al saberlo su pecho quedó helado
su sueño falleció a su costado
el orgullo creció a lo más alto
Y al recorrer el solitario suelo
entre cenizas de campos de batalla
encontró flores forjadas por el viento
nacidas en un negro nido de almas,
negro nido de almas.

('Nido de Almas', Malón 2002[3])

The political crisis[4] of 2001 set the stage for a discussion on the establishment of new subjective positions and the accompanying frameworks of social mobility. The influence of national politics during that period through its deployment of systems of dual power, the delegitimization of bourgeois democracy and its institutions, the deaths hanging over De la Rúa's rule, the violent repression on *Puente Pueyrredón*, and the open debate on the role of cultural actors at the epicenter of the crisis invite a reassessment of the importance of Argentinean heavy metal (particularly as it pertains to its core tendencies, which include *national*[5] tendencies) within the cultural sphere. The strategies adopted by local bands, either to reaffirm or question these core tendencies, exhibit a binary tension. Strategies can either display symbolic tensions (Lorihen, Jason, Renacer, Zeldar) which espouse a glossematic universe with an abstract matrix (words like 'crisis', 'oppression', 'freedom', and 'jail' are foregrounded), or they can exhibit referential tensions (Tren Loco, Horcas, Almafuerte, O'Connor, Serpentor, Harpoon), which promote a glossematic universe with a discursive matrix that emphasizes class awareness (words like 'worker', 'poor', 'laborer', 'marginal', and 'aboriginal' are prevalent).

For the purposes of the present study, we will solely look at those strategies that produce referential tensions. Which social subjects are excluded from this universe? Which discursive formations allow for the discovery of an archeology focused on Argentinean heavy metal's message? To what extent can we assert that nationalist tendencies have expanded the reach of the culturo-musical sphere into other spheres (literature, theater, cinema, politics, history, etc.)?

A *trans*versal look at the material in its totality reveals its undeniable *trans*-disciplinary form. However, when we look at it exclusively as a phenomenon, heavy metal (itself contained within the larger sphere of rock music) demands to be approached as a 'no man's land' (to borrow the title of Riff's 1992 album), a land expanded, traversed, and populated by diverse cultural codes. To ignore its performative character (in the realm of production [poeiesis] this includes musical codes, staging, the live concert's deixis; in the realm of reception, it includes aspects like the pogo dance as a territorial, almost proto-religious ritual) would be absurd. Nevertheless, I would argue that it is in the lyrics where all the codes syncretically converge. Within the lyrics' discursive matrix we will find remnants, marks, and traces of an epochal change. Is it possible that both referential and symbolic strategies display evidence of recurrent discursive formations found in the semantic realm, particularly considering the way these were deployed during Argentina's greatest political, economical, and social crisis, an event that would be followed by the country's return of democracy in 1983?

Such an affirmation would be, at the outset, doubtful. While the political mood of these strategies is established thanks to the interaction of elements present during the era's political situation, there are also other aspects which can be described as cavernous in kind; that is to say, diverse structures and depths (faults,[6] in the sense defined by Néstor Perlongher[7] in 'Caribe Transplatino' 1992) which allow for greater or lesser ambiguity whenever one decides to reflect on, refract, or disrupt the sphere of political aphasia.

In fact, we are reminded of 'looters, time to loot', O'Connor's call to arms voiced in the song 'Nada nos quieren dejar'[8] (*Dolorización*, O'Connor 2002), thus establishing a polarizing vision which seeks to corrode the foundations of the private property ownership philosophy promoted by the highly stratified society prevalent during that epochal December of 2001. That being the case, none of the social actors cast in the crisis reappear in O'Connor's discursive narrative. Within the imaginary matrix I set out to construct and analyze in this chapter, there are subtle aspects worth considering. The first fissure that appears on the structure made up of the tensions considered here is inflicted (it should come as no surprise by now) by Ricardo Iorio with 'Orgullo Argentino', a song found in the album *Piedra Libre* (Iorio 2001). The manifesto voiced at the start of the song calls forth the memory of the looter, of the looted century, in and of itself shaped as a 'memory of centuries'[9]: 'I want to express my Argentinean pride/through this talent for story-telling I inherited/being one of those who doesn't and will never forget/Homeland, Flag, and National pride'. Is not the act of appropriating these symbols, themselves claimed by the bourgeois, effectively an act of individual terrorism?

In its nationalist inflection, this collection of discursive structures similarly reveals some inner contrasts. In Iorio's case, while it is true that the notion of territoriality manifests in his work at a much earlier point than *Piedra Libre* – representing an aspect he systematically explores throughout all of his career (starting with the band Hermética and continuing up to this day) – his approach leaves no space for speculation. The act of looting, as with any other strategy whose purpose is to leave a space barren, functions precisely as an allegorical *shifter*.[10] If we remove a signifier from its original context, which in and of itself is mythological and, one could even argue, ornamental – or was the flag not waving when De la Rúa's helicopter took off from the Rosada?[11] No attention was given to the remains: radicalism[12] had made a revolutionary crisis possible and had opened up a discussion within the traditional bourgeois parties and, simultaneously, within social organizations as far as the practice of democracy was concerned – but again, as I was saying, if we remove a signifier from its original arbitrary connections (signified/signifier) and we synchronically exchange it, we, in effect, imbue it with a history that is Other. (In referencing the Other, we are thinking of Lacan's use of the term, where it signifies an absent or insufficient symbol.)

At this point, let us look at the song 'Crisis' by Horcas (*Horcas* 2002). The song's content can be thought of as referential, but more indefinite in terms of its approach to identity: 'I want to get under your skin and know which side you're on'. The song proposes a particular type of corporeality, or, better yet, a transition from a material body (a body subject to certitude, one that falls under the jurisdiction of Ideological State Apparatuses) to a textual or textural body. In the latter case, even when we 'know which side you're on', the immediacy of the disruption on the regime obstructs any possibility for a social examination. Not even among the social actors who promoted the change – much less within a bipartisan system – was there any tactical certainty or the semblance of a homogeneous body that could respond with a singular blow. In that sense, the matrix of referential structures (beyond the intrinsic differences mentioned above) ordinarily obtains its answers from the meta-collective 'people', all in an effort to (we can only imagine) eliminate the greater problem of class, a problem it clearly finds bothersome or discomforting.

In contrast to the bourgeois approach, Tren Loco has no qualms jumping into the topic of 'class'. Not only is the band disinterested in staking out a particular side on the playing field (that 'side' Horcas demanded) but, in its place, it prefers to delimit a singular detail: the dead accumulated that December become absorbed into the traditions of the labor movement. This thesis finds support in the song 'Pampa del Infierno'[13] (*Ruta 197*, Tren Loco 2002): 'Homicidal handiwork of a foolish king, or not, I can't tell/children of *mind your own business*,[14] representatives of December 20 shout ¡NO!' The result of this intervention is the reestablishment of a tryptic: (1) the political context becomes unavoidable within the cultural realm or any artistic manifestation, for that matter. The artist engages with the social realm because he is an integral part of it; (2) the 'foolish king' intervenes by preaching about a meta-collective movement. What is the place of 'the people', or, better yet, 'the working class', in a bourgeois democracy? This element demands a meditation on the operations undertaken by political parties and those movements associated with the 'popular class' (itself a multi-headed monster seen as representative of a nominal mixture: it is no longer the working class proper, but rather the popular class which comprises the working class); (3) the makeup of the social subject remains unclear, enigmatic, incapable of being located. There are 'piqueteros'.[15] They circulate. They block the highway. They occupy spaces under the constant surveillance of the bourgeois media. They enact the Argentinean left's immanent logic (mainly a Stalinist and Trotskyist logic). Their resistance is harbored under the same lexemes Iorio stole: 'Homeland, Flag and National Pride'. Revolution in Argentina (Santucho[16] rightly pointed out) shares the same tactics found in the international revolution, but it exhibits a strategy all its own. 'Identidad Real', recorded by the band Bloke and released on their record *Demolición* (Bloke 1984), can be offered as another example that aligns with the philosophy presented by Tren Loco as was delineated above: 'I have tried to search for a real identity/not just a mask to show society'. If the subjects who experienced (and served as protagonists in) the 2001 crisis did not find their *modus vivendi* drastically changed, then 20 December must have seemed like a mirage to them.

Lyrics of Rebellion, Without Any Complicities

The emblematic universe I am putting forward here does not imply, necessarily, a recognition of clearly defined, homologous social subjects. Neither can we pretend to argue for an innocuously vulgar naturalism. Nevertheless, it is not beyond the realm of possibility for us to imagine the enunciating subject encountered in these lyrics as a subject defined by stigmas. *Stigma (στίγμα)* can be defined in a broad sense here: as a supernatural mark, as individual punishment (predestined or not), as illness (that which cannot scar or that which is born always already ill, without a cure, mentally *ill*, in-*cure*-able), as a cut without depth, in a sense similar to a tattoo (which is, in fact, its etymological derivative, i.e., to strike and wound). If the 2001/2002 crisis[17] inflicts a wound or a tattoo on the experiential subject (i.e., the enunciating subject), we will have to consider this wound at full volume, connecting it to a genealogy that originates within a different realm (that of literature) which may help us visualize its artistic effects on objects open to observation (i.e., heavy metal lyrics) in the context of a genealogy of wider reach (heavy metal lyrics as literary prosthesis; a space where literature remains beyond reach). By extension, I propose thinking of the wound or the tattoo – as Héctor Libertella suggests in *Nueva Escritura en Latinoamérica* (1977) – as an aesthetic act that elides the life/body of work relation. 'I am what I believe', 'I see but don't believe', 'I believe in what I do': each of these represents axioms offered to us by *Horcas* in their self-titled 2002 album. Belief displaces the document/monument relation (a Foucauldian dyad) as well as the body/mind relation. With this in mind, Ricardo Iorio will express, much later, in 'Unas Estrofas Más'[18] (*Toro y Pampa*, Iorio 2006): 'I will not take the life of my own faith'. In a climate of political skepticism, esotericism directed at the subject is nodal. The ones stigmatized (by stigmatizing themselves) move accompanied by a truth that overtakes the method: marks (whether these are wounds or tattoos) become engraved on their bodies, on their systems of belief, and on their tribes or ghettos. These lyrics (which succumb to a mysticism that aligns to philosophies that promote the intangibility of the Subject), far from being the unifying artifice that brings together the Subject and the lived experience, will claim to have the capacity of de-subjectifying and de-subjetivizing that same Subject. 'This is not a poetry of the self, but of the annihilation of the self' explained Perlongher in the preface to *Caribe Transplatino* (1992). Behind the worrisome assemblage of the deconstructed lyrical 'I', Neo-Baroque's 'dark laboratory' (to use Libertella's expression) 'knits together [...] a weave of rhizomatic allusions and contradictions that transform language into texture' (Perlongher 2008: 95). From the solid to the plastic, or from the solid to the plasmatic; the ectoplasmosis found in the micro-poetic universe of Horcas presents us with two moments: first, a reaction to the lack of social or political references (the system of beliefs migrates to the subject as a 'criollized'[19] dogma originating in the oral tradition)[20] and, second, a replication of violence as a way to restore those references. In both 'Mano Dura'[21] and 'Abre tus Ojos',[22] imaginings of social chaos force the subject to degenerate, to reset, and to rethink itself: 'there go my fists, degeneration'.[23] Violence instinctively rehabilitates a hollowed-out subject. A similar characterization can be found in O'Connor's *Dolorización*[24] (from the similarly titled album 2002): 'My poor, poor generation, lost in darkness/people who feel alone and die while cooped up'. Is the version of 'Eleanor Rigby' in *Dolorización* just an unrelated expression of this same desire? All those '[...] lonely people' condensed and crammed into the legend (legend or physical person?, we will never know) imagined by McCartney in *Revolver* (The Beatles 1966): 'All the lonely people/Where do they all come from?' The Eleanor narrativized by The Beatles was a maid who worked at a hospital located in the city of Parkhill. In the local equivalent, Roberto Arlt[25] had created a miserabilist prototype (as Boedo's poets would put it; Arlt was counted among their ranks) in his play *300 Millones* (1927), itself based on a journalistic account. However, in contrast to Eleanor, Arlt's maid commits suicide. Can we argue that McCartney follows the tradition of Conrad, while Arlt follows Dostoevsky? These represent lineages that, luckily, we will never be able to pinpoint.

With regards to Horcas, their apparent lack of reflectiveness as far as Power is concerned ('Power' capitalized here on account of its identitarian aspirations, given that there is no Deleuzian influence in sight) is of note: 'the solution, rebellion/times are difficult/impossible not to fight back/they want to see us dead/ will power ever run out?' OK, but, what exactly is Power in this syntagmatic structure posed by Horcas? Power, in this conception, represents a medieval anthropomorphism that functions as a stand in of the enemy, so long as the enunciating subject suffers from its stigmatizing effects. Nonetheless, the rebellion (another imprecise lexematic fiction that presupposes a state of dignity, the ability to name oneself in the midst of institutional chaos) has unimaginable limits. The band Visceral captures this sentiment in the song 'Arrancado del Sistema'[26] (Visceral 2000): 'choosing between waiting or setting off,/accepting either punishment or rebellion'. Lyrics such as 'Marginal' by Harpoon or 'Rezo a la Indiferencia'[27] by Claudio O'Connor express analogous consequences. We take in the 'blow of the horn'[28] (to borrow Claudio's poetry), the inevitable, the imaginary revolutionary origin of violence, when parliaments become bogged down in compromises and decay. Violence remains the basis of the everyday (always in the Benjaminian sense). It moves out of the legal sphere to consider other expressions of violence, of rage. Rage is not a means to an end, but a manifestation, and, as such, it remains apart from other considerations. In 1981, Riff sang the following: 'Aggressive, without a motive/what goes through my mind is of no importance' (*Ruedas de Metal*, Riff 1981). The incitement to violence promoted by Riff's brand of hard rock, with its chains and black leather jacket iconography, implied an escape, a cutting loose, a freedom for those who were being overlooked and marginalized.

The 20 December 2001, enacted several forms of violence, hooliganisms that went against the grain (as Roberto Carri has taught us). In *Ruta 197* (Tren Loco 2002),[29] Tren Loco proposed breaking away from Horcas' traditional positioning and, instead, assume the position (suspended, forgotten, overlooked) of the working class through an irreducible Peronist histogram. 'Fuera de la Ley'[30] exhibits all the pestilent elements of the Ida del Gaucho Martín Fierro, the Cuban Revolution, the 'piquetero' movement, and Evita Capitana (a libertarian melange not suitable for present-day sociology, or *sociodism*, a term I invented with Oscar Blanco in our work about rock lyrics, to taxonomize the purveyors of the origin myths, miscellany, collections of anecdotes, and statistics about that atrocious lie some call 'National Rock').

The burden of antagonism between rich and poor, bourgeois and proletarian, boss and worker, is transferred to, at least in Tren Loco's lyrics, on other types of entities: on the immigrant, the illiterate peasant, the territorial popular movements, the unionized worker; in short, on a 'criollo reality' that moves from the gauchesca to the feuilleton, from Boedist miserabilism to Marechal's[31] Dantesque mysticism, opening up spaces of convergence and dissension which are driven by the only motivator of the industrialization of (late) desire in the Río de la Plata: the trail of hunger. Hunger mobilizes, transforms, destroys, annihilates; it perverts identities and the main risks found in the act of enunciation; it heightens the animalistic adrenalin that overwhelms those persecuted by the repressive forces of the State: 'persecuted for some change/the father and good husband runs away/nonetheless, the people/suspect him of being a hoodlum' (*Ruta 197*, Tren Loco 2002). The lyrics evince sentiments of bewilderment, the distrust directed at the supposed civilizing character of the modern (developmental) State, an institution that likes to paint itself as responsible for industrializing and bearing the weight of a guiding morality. The discussion concerning the political and economical destiny of the country transforms into a discussion about the unbreakable bond between Nation and territory, State and citizenry, social subjects and regulatory structures. Of course, the menemist vision (of a degenerate welfare State) has a forceful influence on the following fragment: 'they burned Evita's work down/while wearing the costume of freedom'. The mythological unveiling of the 'productive revolution' of the 1990s reproduces mottoes of documentary veracity: this (pure deixis) IS NOT Peronism. However, this relation based on truth (what is and what is not, in line with Foucault: what can and can't be read as a Peronist, returning to the notion of the *archive*) between the workers movement and its natural direction (at the heart of Justicialismo[32]) becomes distorted between Cutral-Có[33] and the date 20 December 2001. In the song 'Pampa del Infierno' the lyrical content resembles a propaganda pamphlet: 'it is time to turn the ox around'. But this is not the disgraced, melancholic and depoliticized 'ox' found in A.N.I.M.A.L.'s 'Lejos de Casa', the impactful second cut of *El Nuevo Camino del Hombre* (A.N.I.M.A.L. 1996); on the contrary, this is an 'ox' carrying historical marks: carrying the bureaucratic direction of a syndicalist Peronism and the vertical direction of the dismantled political subjects (both of these representing the two-party system: radicals and Peronists). The political tradition of the Argentinean people (a tradition at once deified, mythologized, canonized, and even caricatured) forces both Tren Loco and Harpoon, the latter in their song 'Piqueteando' (*Batalla Eterna*, Harpoon 2006) – both during a period subsequent to the focus of this chapter – to think about an autonomist movement with territorial reach mired in its own Peronist traditions. It also forces them to think about the popular left and/or even about the most radical (though delayed in their picketing practices) sectors of the Trotskyite left: in other words, what we have in mind, of course, is the Partido Obrero. The 'Pampa from Hell' does not refer, it should be obvious, to the Napalpí territory in our Chaco Province; that much is clear. The histrionic gesture of Illia Kuryaki & The Valderramas in their 1995 album *Chaco*, which helped fertilize a politically and touristically dead territory, and the kitschy offerings of Babasónicos in their 1999 *Miami*,[34] which served as a strategic denouncement of the menemate's dismantling, have nothing to do with Tren Loco's referential vindication in what became a wildly successful imaginary pseudo-filial connection (I do not mean to be sarcastic when stating this; not at all): the labor movement has what could be seen as natural empathy, or perhaps we should say naturalized empathy, due to its British roots?) with heavy metal. This was Maristella Svampa's aim in 'Identidades Astilladas; De la Patria Metalúrgica al Heavy Metal'[35] (2000a). Svampa's interpretation is linear and lacks some cohesion (the project is an amalgam between a union-based movement, unaffiliated to Peronist ideals, that was emerging in the late 1990s and a combative anti-establishment brand of heavy metal whose message was developing a nationalist tone), but it does push the envelop in terms of thinking about the reshaping of imaginable subjectivities, to an extent being ahead of the curve by looking forward to what would develop during the 2001 crisis. Fundamentally, the project considers what it sees as the 'erosion of identity' in the country's youth, as manifested within Buenos Aires' metal community; a community which, far from yielding to skepticism and inertia, helped strengthen the workers' critical awareness and its attendant struggle against union bureaucracy.

That being the case, we must also consider a different segment within the youth, that segment that is not part of labor's activist segment, but which, nonetheless, has undertaken a major leap in its class consciousness. In 'Rostro Oscuro',[36] Tren Loco conjures up the Christ-like image (a non-guerrilla Christ, from the south of Greater Buenos Aires, not from La Higuera) of Darío Santillán, who was murdered while wearing a Hermética t-shirt[37]; Maximiliano Kosteki also comes to mind in this process. Ariel Hendler, Mariano Pacheco, and Juan Rey note in their book

Darío Santillán: El Militante que Puso Cuerpo[38] (2012) that while Darío was reading Gambini's Che Guevara biography, he was also listening to 'Atravesando todo Límite'. We must commend the authors for including a selection of lyrics (written by Ana Mourín, it must be noted) and, in doing so, communicating the significant role national heavy metal played among the militant student neighborhoods located in Greater Buenos Aires. Nevertheless, and being as honest as we can be, we must also note that this sampling of referential tensions associated with a nationalist revolutionary tendency (Blanco and Scaricaciottoli 2014b: 329) exhibits inherently deep contradictions: from the 'chorrito sorete'[39] of 'Niño Jefe'[40] (Almafuerte 1998) to the 'Maldito Punga'[41] of Serpentor (Serpentor 2001) there seems to be a shared belief in the vindicating nature of slum hooliganism, but, at the same time, a particular intolerance projected toward marginal delinquency, toward the lumpen pickpocket, toward the petty thief who sets shop at the local station. In 'Sirva Otra Vuelta Pulpero'[42] (Almafuerte's version of a Cuchilla Grande song, recorded for the album *Piedra Libre*) the territorial takeover on the part of 'undocumented' individuals is defended in a redemptive (and, one could argue, Christian) manner by a humanism that, ultimately, directs power against a public force: 'that is why with just eleven families/we have for once defeated the State'. The same Iorio, who condemns the use given by the 'piquetero' movement of the gerund 'cheguevareando'[43] in his *Toro y Pampa* (2006) as well as in several public statements, the latter pointless for this chapter, is ultimately trumped by his own rhetoric.

On This Side of the Mirror

There is a photo shot by Lewis Carroll, which has had very little circulation. It is a well-known fact that Carroll was very interested in photography (in addition to mirrors and holes) and, particularly, photography associated with infancy. The B-side of literary criticism has deployed the word pedophilia to speak of this photo. I choose the A-side; the word that comes to mind is desire. The photo in question was taken in the year 1858 and the person in it is the real-life Alice, or, perhaps we should say, her alter ego: Alice Liddell. One could ask who is who, which is the real Alice and which is the fictional one. What is known is that Carroll and Alice were friends in the bleak 'village' of Oxford during the mid-nineteenth century. My interest in the photo has nothing to do with addressing issues of authenticity. We will leave that to Magritte. By now we all know it is not a pipe. My attention focuses on the handicapped, deprived, and cornered body of Alice Liddell. The image seems to me much more preferable than to alternately think of the girl that becomes trapped in the rabbit's room and disappoints the *gore-loving* reader – which we all have within – by not being decapitated. That attraction is the reference's simulacrum; to know that her name is tied to a wonderful tale, in order to come back to her, the girl in the photo, only to be denied the playing of cards, the trials, and the caterpillars. Instead, we only gain access to the gray concrete of the walls, the wrinkled clothing, the lost gaze, and that inexplicable anguish.

There is, to a certain extent, an excess in the *corpus* of poetics that have reflected on the 2001 crisis. It is an aesthetic excess: the harshness, the violence, and the irreconcilable gesture of heavy metal music are imbued with sensibility upon recognizing the need to think of, reflect on, and intervene with death. In the writings of Zavala or Iorio himself – the latter whose face Darío Santillán displayed on a t-shirt in a now-equally iconographic image – the dead of 20 December become the irreversible profusion of excess, a hyper-realism that compels us to reassess an artistic body of work. Who is the 'real' Iorio? The one displayed on Darío's and many other youths' t-shirts, the ones who found in Hermética a reason to get involved in social militancy? Or is he the one who traverses life 'cheguevariando?' The fact that the nationalist brand of heavy metal has focused on the goings-on of a country that finds itself up in flames speaks, in and of itself, of a movement (hopefully the General does not mind this usage[44]) that, at least regarding the tensions considered here, has deposed the dragon, the unicorn, and even Alice herself, but achieving this from the other side of the mirror. I echo my own words and reading in 'Linajes y rupturas de una imaginación humanista. Almafuerte, Castelnuovo, Iorio'[45] (2012): 'We must mine the social realm and literature as tools (*iron, lead, trigger*[46]) to correct the course of an imagination that has been restrained, placated, segmented in the parking lot'.

REFERENCES

Agamben, Giorgio (2008), *Signatura Rerum, Sobre el método*, Barcelona: Anagrama.

A.N.I.M.A.L. (1996), *El Nuevo Camino del Hombre*, CD, Argentina: Warner Music.

Almafuerte (1998), *Almafuerte*, CD, Argentina: Interdisc.

——— (2001), *Piedra Libre*, CD, Argentina: Universal.

——— (2006), *Toro y Pampa*, CD, Argentina: Dejesu.

——— (2012), *Trillando la Fina*, CD, Argentina: Dejesú.

Babasónicos (1999), *Miami*, CD, Argentina: Sony Music.

Batalla Eterna (2006), *Harpoon*, CD, Argentina: Hurling Metal Records.

Blanco, Oscar and Scaricaciottoli, Emiliano (2014a), *Las Letras de Rock en Argentina. De la Caída de la Dictadura a la Crisis de la Democracia (1983–2001)*, Buenos Aires: Colihue.

——— (2014b), 'Noventas alternativos', in *Las letras de Rock en Argentina. De la Caída de la Dictadura a la Crisis de la Democracia (1983–2001)*, Buenos Aires: Colihue, pp. 40–190.

Bloke (1984), *Demolición*, CD, Argentina: Umbral Discos.
Hendler, Ariel, Pacheco, Mariano, and Rey, Juan (2012), *Darío Santillán. El Militante que Puso el Cuerpo*, Buenos Aires: Planeta.
Horcas (2002), *Horcas*, CD, Argentina: El Pie Registros.
Illya Kuryaki and The Valderramas (1995), *Chaco*, CD, Argentina: Gigoló Productions.
Libertella, Héctor (1977), *Nueva Escritura en Latinoamérica*, Caracas: Monte Ávila.
Malón (1996), *Justicia o Resistencia*, CD, Argentina: Odeon.
Minore, Gito (2010), *Tren Loco. 20 Años. Pogo en el Andén*, Buenos Aires: Yugular Records.
Minore, Gito, Calvo, Manuela, and Scaricaciottoli, Emiliano (2014), 'La recepción de Iorio en la Academia', in *Cultura Metálica*, Buenos Aires: Clara Beter, pp. 23–38.
O'Connor (2002), *Dolorización*, CD, Argentina: Tocka Discos.
Perlongher, Néstor (1992), 'Caribe transplatino', *Revista La Caja*, n° 1, pp. 9–21.
——— (2008), *Prosa Plebeya: Ensayos 1980–1992*, Buenos Aires: Colihue.
Riff (1981), *Ruedas de Metal*, CD, Argentina: Tonodisc/ATC.
Scaricaciottoli, Emiliano (2012), 'Linajes y rupturas de una imaginación humanista: Almafuerte, Castelnuovo, Iorio', in M. Vitagliano (ed.), *Boedo: Políticas del Realismo,* Buenos Aires: Título, pp. 10–25.
Serpentor (2001), *Serpentor*, CD, Argentina: Kirkincho Records.
Svampa, Maristella (2000a), 'Identidades astilladas. De la Patria metalúrgica al heavy metal', in M. Svampa (ed.), *Desde Abajo: Las Transformaciones de las Identidades Sociales*, Buenos Aires: Biblos, pp. 121–55.
——— (2000b), *Desde Aabajo: Las Transformaciones de las Identidades Sociales*, Buenos Aires: Biblos.
The Beatles (1966), *Revolver*, Vinyl, Argentina: Capitol Records.
Tren Loco (2002), *Ruta 197*, CD, Argentina: Yugular Records.
Visceral (2000), *Arrancado del Sistema*, CD, Argentina: Vampyr Discos.

NOTES

1. Reference to the title of an *Almafuerte* album, it is also an expression used in the game of hide-and-seek, particularly when one of the players in the role of hiding gains access to home base while remaining unseen. Upon reaching home base the player yells 'piedra libre', thus freeing all other players from being caught. One English equivalent is 'Olly, Olly, Oxen free!' (t/n).
2. We have retained this phrase in Spanish because the word 'ablande' carries a multitude of meanings, all of which are relevant to the present chapter. One way to translate it could be 'Strategies to Avert a Weakening'. The idea of 'ablande' is frequently used as a counterpoint to the concept of 'aguante', which is a polysemic word used in Argentinian metal to express solidarity, and sometimes, political agency. Nevertheless, such a literal translation would ignore the author's allusions to other matters relevant to the chapter (t/n).

3. Reflected in childhood's sadness
a dream died in each adventure
somewhere between his innocence and cries
he grew up consumed in his existence
As a grown-up he searched for the answer
when he found it, his chest froze
his dream perished at his side
pride grew tall
And while roaming the lonely land
amongst the ashes strewn on the battlefield
he discovered flowers forged by the wind
born in a black den of souls, a black den of souls
(t/n)

4. The 2001 Argentinean crisis was a popular uprising meant as a response to the political, social and economic meltdown which brought down the government of Fernando de la Rúa and resulted in a power vacuum. The protests were met with repressive force on the part of the State, causing the death of many (t/n).
5. See 'Tendencia nacionalista revolucionaria' in Blanco, Oscar and Scaricaciottoli, Emiliano. *Las letras del rock en Argentina. De la caída de la dictadura a la crisis de la democracia (1983–2001)*. Buenos Aires, Colihue, 2014. For a closer look at the nationalist tendencies in the figure of Ricardo Iorio, refer to the trajectory I develop in 'Linajes y rupturas de una imaginación humanista' in Vitagliano, Miguel (Comp.) *Boedo. Políticas del Realismo*. Buenos Aires Título, 2012. Likewise, and finally, I recommend referring to the round table organized by Gito Minore (editor of Clara Beter and member of GIIHMA) for the I Heavy Metal Book Fair of Buenos Aires, in which we participated with Nuna Calvo, 'La Recepción de Iorio en la Academia', Cultura Metálica, Buenos Aires, Clara Beter, 2014.
6. 'Tajos' carries with it two meanings: first, the idea of a fault, like the ones found between the continents under water; second, the notion of a gash or a cut inflicted on something. I have chose the word 'fault' given its greater alignment with the sense pertaining to depths (t/n).
7. Argentinian poet, writer, and one of the founders of the Frente de Liberación Homosexual (Homosexual Liberation Front) in 1971 (t/n).
8. 'They Won't Leave a Thing to Us' (t/n).
9. Reference to Hermética's album, *Memoria de siglos* (t/n).
10. For more on this, see Roman Jakobson.
11. Reference to the notorious moment during the 2001 Argentinean crisis when then-president Fernando de la Rúa abdicated and abandoned the Casa Rosada (Argentinean official residence or Government House), making his escape by helicopter in the midst of ongoing riots and acts of repression occurring on the streets.

12. 'Radicalismo': Here the word pertains to the Unión Cívica Radical (Radical Civic Union), the oldest Argentinean political party, still active to this day.
13. 'Pampa from Hell' (t/n).
14. 'No te metas': Colloquial idiom meaning 'mind your own business'. In Argentina, it carries a strong connotation which refers to the implicit attitude that a large sector of the civil society adopted during the last dictatorship, when news of the disappeared, tortured, and executed people began to circulate (t/n).
15. 'Piqueteros'. Picketing as a form of protest took hold in Argentina during the 1990s and grew to become a full-fledged social movement: the *movimiento piquetero*. I have opted to keep the Spanish word to distinguish between this phenomenon in Argentina and its various iterations elsewhere (t/n).
16. Mario Roberto Santucho, Argentinian revolutionary, founder of the Partido Revolucionario de los Trabajadores. Disappeared in an act of state terrorism in 1976 (t/n).
17. We must make it clear that we are not concerned here with discussing the socio-political reach of the crisis within the bourgeois democratic system but, rather, the wealth of allusions captured by the lyrics through the production of a micro-poetics during the two years in consideration.
18. 'A Few More Stanzas' (t/n).
19. That is to say, native, with a particular rural and folkloric inflection (t/n).
20. Let us call to mind Iorio's artistic choices in 'Por Ser Yo' and 'Amanecer en Open Door' (both found in *Piedra Libre*, 2001). In the first case, we encounter an intra-text: 'I am the one who in the past sang 'Be Yourself'/Today because I am myself, I travel errantly'. To travel errantly is no longer the act of a fugitive, it is not the roaming of one who chooses to be 'Outside the Law' (Tren Loco), but rather it is the disconcerted roaming of one who has 'navigated' a path of solitude to the exclusion of the system's control apparatuses. As stated by Agamben in *Signatura Rerem* (2008), even without power (that is to say, will to power), the *panopticon* is not a dream building but a diagram of the mechanism of power in its ideal form; a singular object that defines the intelligibility of the mechanism to which it belongs to which at the same time it shapes. What happens to those not yet committed? The non-committed, the undefined, ('el perro cristiano' [a reference to Iorio: t/n], without going any further) fall into a different realm, that of the insane asylum. The latter is the second case, between parodic and desperate (at the end of the song Iorio shouts 'Doctor, doctor' as a children choir rules 'Mad, mad, mad'). In 'Amanecer en Open Door', the subject gives up his ontological condition and (be)comes lost within the logos of a civilizing hygienist realm: the ones who are anomalous or monstrous are sent to the madhouse. Monstrosity, in this sense, depends on how remote one is in relation to the light. Darkness is tantamount to a loss of visibility which isolation introduces regarding the objects in its vicinity. But monstrosity does not always seek to isolate itself in the hygienist panopticon. In 'Die monster, die' (*Trillando la Fina*, 2013) it is precisely the enunciating subject who, by reaffirming his illness (science could not cure him) while in a wide open country territory

(a few kilometers south of Open Door) will remove the monster from the neighborhood. Iorio vs. Alien (a movable parasitic brand of escapism). The monster Iorio defines (signs) in this song as the immanent absence of the sign: if you cannot confront the impossibility of naming yourself, die. The madman, the one captured in Open Door, is the only one who can refer to himself (the one who sang 'Sé Vos', wandered errantly, was denied by science, and now faces escapism, representing a delayed humanism, a nostalgic Quixote of the rural utopia). Paradoxes.

21. 'Hand of Steel' (t/n).
22. 'Open Your Eyes' (t/n).
23. See what happens with the 'D-Generation' of Babasónicos (*Pasto*, 1992) in the menemist incipit. For that: Blanco, Oscar and Scaricaciottoli, Emiliano. 'Noventas Alternativos' in Las letras de rock en Argentina. De la caída de la dictadura a la crisis de la democracia (1983–2001). Buenos Aires, Colihue, 2014.
24. 'Dolorization': Neologism meant to convey the act of making something painful (t/n).
25. Argentinian writer and journalist who was part of the Boedo group, a literary group of great influence in Buenos Aires during the first decades of the twentieth century (t/n).
26. 'Torn from the System' (t/n).
27. 'A Prayer to Indifference' (t/n).
28. Reference to Argentinean newspaper 'Clarín' which is owned by a right-wing media corporation (t/n).
29. The only reputable study on the life and work of *Tren Loco* is the voluptuous and ambitious work by Gito Minore: *Tren Loco. 20 Años. Pogo en el Andén*. Buenos Aires, Ygular Records, 2010.
30. 'Outside the Law' (t/n).
31. Leopoldo Marechal, another prominent writer related to the Florida literary group, an faction opposed to the Boedo group (t/n).
32. 'Justicialismo', philosophy of the Justicialist Party, heir to the original Peronist Party (t/n).
33. Between 1996 and 1997, a series of large popular uprisings took place in the cities of Cutral-Có and Plaza Huincul, which targeted the neoliberal policies of menemism. It was the origin of the 'piquetero' movement (t/n).
34. The album boasted a cover, which presented the Floridian peninsula; however, upon turning the cover 90 degrees counterclockwise, the peninsula became the Argentinian littoral.
35. 'Splintered identities: From the Metallurgic Homeland to Heavy Metal' (t/n).
36. 'Dark Face' (t/n).
37. Close attention should be paid to the hierarchy displayed in the most widely disseminated photo of Darío Santillán, set at a protest undertaken by high school students at the San Francisco Solano school, during a time when he was an active member of the Agrupación 11 de Julio (a document in which, thanks to the help of the Santillán family, the above-mentioned authors depicted in page 194 of the book). Darío walks with his back toward the demonstration as he flashes a wonderful smile. Displayed on Darío's chest, Ricardo Iorio is

depicted four or five heads higher than his ex-bandmates from *Hermética*. Indio Solari was absolutely wrong when he stated 'Nobody will listen to your t-shirt anymore': this is not a short-lived fad; the presence of national heavy metal in the iconography of the popular, labor, and class movements of the late twentieth century is tangential.

38. 'Darío Santillán: The Activist Who Put His Body on the Line' (t/n).
39. 'Little Thieving Shit' (t/n).
40. 'Boss Kid' (t/n).
41. 'Damned Pickpocket' (t/n).
42. 'Bartender, Another Round' (t/n).
43. Cheguevariando: neologism that uses the name of Che Guevara to describe the act of fronting or projecting a certain strength and attitude, in a type of imitation of Che Guevara, that is ultimately unaccompanied by any substance.
44. General Juan Domingo Perón, who adopted the signifier 'movement' as one of the core concepts of his political creation. There is some tongue-in-cheek irony with this remark on the part of the author (t/n).
45. 'Lineages and Ruptures of a Humanist Imagination: Almafuerte, Castelnuovo, Iorio' (t/n).
46. Words intended to convey the language of firearms (t/n).

Notes on Contributors

EZEQUIEL ALASIA is a student of language and literature at the University of Bueno Aires; Audiovisual production (CIEVYC), and the director and scriptwriter of the film *La Secta: Una Película por Desobediencia Civil.* He contributed to the book on Ricky Poesia, *Nunca Seré Poesía,* with the article 'Nunca nos fuimos pero volvimos porque no entendiste lo que te dijeron'. Alasia was also the sound technician, cameraman, musician, poetry and short story writer for *Acción Mutante: Terrorismo Literario* and *Cuadernos de la Fisura.*

* * * * *

MANUEL BERNAL is a professor with a degree in communications from the University of Bueno Aires. Born in Suipacha, he spends his days traveling between his birthplace and Buenos Aires. Bernal was also the guitarist of the band Cienbarrios for several years, the director of *Vuelan Chanchos* and has previously written for *El Zordo.*

* * * * *

DIEGO CABALLERO is a professor in communication sciences at the University of Buenos Aires and a high school teacher. He is also the enthusiastic host of *El Club de los Intolerantes* (Radio Lexia). Caballeri has written articles on music for the magazines *Alrededores, El Zordo* and the website Marcha.

* * * * *

GITO MINORE studied philosophy at the University of Buenos Aires where he edited several books of poetry and prose fiction. In 2010 he published the book

Tren Loco 20 Años: Pogo en el Andén, a history of the mythical band from Greater Buenos Aires, now in its second edition. Since 2013, Minore has organized the Heavy Metal Book Fair in Buenos Aires and its provinces. For some years now he has run the Clara Beter publishing house that has published, among others, the book *Cultura Metálica 1 y 2*, which gathers the presentations and debates that take place at the fairs. He has also participated in several book fairs and literature meetings in Argentina and abroad.

* * * * *

Daniel Nevárez Araújo holds a doctorate in comparative literature from the University of Massachusetts, as well as an MA in English literature and Bachelor's in accounting from the University of Puerto Rico. Nevárez Araújo has published essays on topics ranging from comedy and disabilities, to the poetics of documentary and the medical humanities. He has also served as assistant translation editor for the *Massachusetts Review*. More recently, he has collaborated with Nelson Varas-Díaz as translator, co-editor and consultant in various documentary features and published works.

* * * * *

Juan Ignacio Pisano holds a doctorate in literature from the Department of Philosophy and Literatures at the University of Buenos Aires. His doctoral thesis is entitled 'Ficciones de Pueblo. Comunidad, Plebe y Poesía Gauchesca (1776–1835)'. He has published essays on topics such as gauchesca poetry, science fiction, Latin American colonial literature and Argentinean literature. He has also taught at both the middle school and college levels. Additionally, he has published various works of fiction, including the novel *El Último Falcón Sobre la Tierra* (Baltasara Editora 2019).

* * * * *

Emiliano Scaricaciottoli teaches literary theory at UBA and nineteenth-century Argentinean narratives at UNA. He edited the first two books put out by GIIHMA: *Se Nos Ve de Negro Vestidos: Siete Enfoques sobre el Heavy Metal Argentino* (La Parte Maldita 2016; republished in a second edition in 2017) and *Parricidas: Mapa Rabioso del Metal Argentino Contemporáneo* (La Parte Maldita 2018). Additionally, he co-authored (along with Oscar Blanco) the book *Las Letras de Rock en Argentina: De la Caída de la Dictadura a la Crisis de la Democracia (1983–2001)* (Colihue 2014). Along with Mauro Petrillo he co-wrote *Las Cosas que Te Digo No Repitas Jamás: La Palabra de la Mujer en el Rock* (Disconario 2018) and *Toma el Tren hacia el Sur: Postales de Voces Extremas* (Disconario-CronosRock 2019).

Scaricaciottoli contributed to the first two editions of *Cultura Metálica* (Clara Beter 2014/2015) and in a collection edited by Miguel Vitagliano Boedo entitled *Políticas del Realismo* (Título 2012). He has written for *El Zordo, Marcha, Anden Digital* and *La Luna con Gatillo*. Finally, he has acted as representative of GIIHMA in the *Colectivo de Investigación y Acción desde el Metal de Habla Hispana* (CIAMHH).

* * * * *

Luciano Scarrone, a self-taught musician since age 14, has participated in several rock and heavy metal projects. In 2004 he began a bachelor's degree in arts and culture management at the Universidad Nacional de Tres de Febrero (UNTREF) and he is currently developing his thesis about the current state of the market and the Argentinean heavy metal scene. He has published articles on the Argentinean heavy metal scene and market in the news website Marcha and for the newspaper *Andén*.

* * * * *

Gustavo Torreiro is a graduate and professor of middle and higher education in political science at the University of Buenos Aires. Torrreiro is currently working as a high school teacher in Buenos Aires Province. He has published articles in several publications.

* * * * *

Nelson Varas-Díaz is a professor of social-community psychology at Florida International University's Department of Global and Sociocultural Studies. His work related to metal music addresses issues of community formation, linkages between culture and music and metal music as a decolonial strategy in Latin America. His work has been published in multiple journals, including *Metal Music Studies*, *International Journal of Community Music* and the *Journal of Community Psychology*, among others. He coedited the book *Heavy Metal Music and the Communal Experience.* He also produced and/or directed the award-winning documentaries *The Distorted Island: Heavy Metal and Community in Puerto Rico*, *The Metal Islands: Culture, History and Politics in Caribbean Metal Music*, and *Songs of Injustice: Heavy Metal Music in Latin America*. Together, the films have garnered more than 30 sets of laurels in international film festivals. He is one of the editors of the *Metal Music Studies* journal published by Intellect. He currently directs the 'Heavy Metal Studies – Latin America' group which researches metal in the Caribbean, Central and South America.

Index

www.ingramcontent.com/pod-product-compliance
Lightning Source LLC
LaVergne TN
LVHW060728310826
846742LV00016B/56
9781789387483